Published in 1984 by Osprey Publishing Limited
12—14 Long Acre, London WC2E 9LP
Member of the George Philip Group

Produced by the staff of Trucking International
Förlags AB Albinsson & Sjöberg, Box 23
371 21 Karlskrona, Sweden
for Förlagshuset Norden AB
Box 305, 201 23 Malmö, Sweden

British Library in Cataloguing Publication Data

Bergendahl, Sture
Trucking around the world
   1. Trucks
   I. Title   II. Sjöberg, Stig
629.2'24   TL230
ISBN 0-85045-601-0

Printed in Italy

TRUCKING
AROUND THE WORLD

by the staff of Trucking International

Edited by Sture Bergendahl
Stig Sjöberg

CONTENTS

chapter 1

AUSTRALIAN ROADTRAINS

Australia is more than just a country; it's an entire continent, as large as the USA and Alaska put together. Distances between cities and 'towns' are enormous, which creates huge difficulties for the haulage industry.

45 per cent of the continent consists of fruitless desert in which the railway network is poorly developed. Truckers carry 80 per cent of all goods.

Only in the eastern parts of the country can the railways compete effectively with the trucking industry. And effective it has been. Truckers are forced to compete on the railways' terms, resulting in huge deficits each year for the trucking industry.

Along the coastal regions, especially in the south-east, the laws are tough on the trucking community. In the other parts of Australia, however, more flexibility, with an eye to industrial relations for the hauliers, is used in the law-making process.

Several states allow 'roadtrains' up to 45 meters in lenght, with total weights of up to 120—130 tonnes. But roadtrains weighing in at 150 tonnes are common.

During 1979, new legislation made gross weights of up to 38 tonnes possible in all states. This came about after nine days of strikes by about 3000 one-rig owner-operators. They parked their rigs along highways into the major cities, blocking all traffic until the authorities raised the maximum weight allowed.

One-rig operators are important to Australia. But current legislation treats them less fairly when compared to other groups in society. To top it all they are not covered by the 'ordinary' consumer-protection laws, since they are private businessmen!

For example, if a trucker gets his rig repaired and the workmanship is substandard, the shop owner can tell the trucker to 'get lost' if the trucker lays claim. The only recourse is to sue — if he's got the money. Whithout watertight evidence his chances of winning the case are slim.

(Left) A roadtrain snakes its way through a serpentine mountain pass. With this heavy load, climbing these slopes becomes extremely demanding on both rig and driver.

Over: Preparing to roll. A roadtrain being readied to transport cattle through the desert. Men and cattle will have to survive the heat. A fully loaded two trailer 'train' can weigh as much as 130 tonnes.

AUSTRALIAN ROADTRAINS

Many laws regarding commercial traffic date from 1933. An example is workhour limitation which require that a trucker rest six hours during a 24 hour shift.

Weight regulations are stiff; over 40,000 truckers are convicted for excessive loads each year. The owner or the director, is responsible for all fines.

One of the foundations of Australian weight legislation is the American 'bridge-formula', which benefits American-type rigs that have the front axle placed well forward.

American rigs are the most common. They came to Australia in 1962 when a trucker imported five Kenworths directly from the USA and put them into service between Sydney and Melbourne. Other truckers followed suit and soon the Kenworth was an everyday sight on Australian roads.

The American rigs are, despite their capacity, very light. In Australia they are equipped, as are many others, with fibreglass sleeping-cabins. In many cases the cabs are made completely of fibreglass. A local plant makes Mack cabs this way.

Other makes had to improvize. Scania, for example, was forced to swich to a single-frame chassis on their tractor units. The heavy tandem rear axle package was exchanged for the lighter American

AUSTRALIAN ROADTRAINS

model, a so called 'four-feather bogie'. The front axle was moved forward almost 50 cm, and the rigs were equipped with the commonly used 'wire-spoke' wheels. Today Scania is one of the top sellers.

Before the American breakthrough, British Leyland, Australian built International and the German Mercedes were the top models. Today Australia is considered to be one of the world's toughest truck markets, with all the big names represented.

There are trucks from the USA, Europe and Japan. Most of them are assembled within the country due to import restrictions, which protects employment at home.

There are also domestic makes on the market, the biggest being Leader, formed in 1962. It looks like a Mack, since the cabs are actually made by Mack. RFW, formed in 1969 and originally equipped with Scania engines, is also represented. Tiger is a newcomer built by a large trucking company to fit their specific needs. Chassis and cab come from Germany's MAN organization, while the engine and other parts of the powertrain come from American factories.

The most common combination here as in Europe, is a tractor unit with a three-axled trailer. The only difference being that in Australia tractors almost always

(Above) En route home. Empty trailers play 'piggy-back' while the rigs fight their way through dirt and sand.

Over: Fully loaded, this convoy hauls vital equipment to a desert site.

AUSTRALIAN ROADTRAINS

have three axles. The trailer axles are usually equipped with twin tyres, which gives 8.5 tonnes axle weight against 5.4 tonnes with single-tyres.

In the inter-city traffic one can see beautifully finished and equipped rigs; the Aussies aren't far behind the Americans.

The climate makes it easy to keep a rig looking good with the bright sunlight giving extra glitter to the chrome, except when the rig hits the dirt tracks. Signs and company logos are applied with cautious diligence.

One fifth of all the vehicles in Australia are trucks — in total, that's 1.2 million! Every year, no-expenses spared are trucking shows and fairs — big attractions with the populace.

Roadtrains are something genuinely Australian. Lengths of up to 45 meters and weights of up to 150 tonnes seem to be sheer lunacy. But seen through local eyes such rules are sensible as well as necessary.

As much as 80 per cent of the country's total flow goes by truck. One must remain aware of economies of scale especially when distances run are usually between 1000 and 3000 kilometers.

The law permits two trailers per tractor unit or three trailers behind a rigid truck. These 'dogs' as they are called, are often 12.5 meters units with three or five axles.

But normally, an additional two or three trailers are tacked on anyway. The further into the 'outback' one goes, the longer and heavier these roadtrains get. In any case, the truckers regard the law as very flexible. One drives under the banner 'Nobody's guilty until he's caught'!

Every roadtrain has to have a special permit from the police authorities. On the application, such items as route of length, engine type and displacement, number of axles, wheels and trailers are stated, as well as type of goods being carried. After the authorities give the 'OK', the driver always has to have a copy of the permit in the cab. to be shown to the police if needed.

The chances of the police being able to effectively control overloads, improper registrations or normal traffic flow in the vastness of the desert are practically non-existent.

The roadtrains of the 'outback' supply the needs of the people: foodstuff, household goods, hardware, fuel, building materials, even prefab housing!

One of their biggest markets is livestock transportation. It was for this reason that the roadtrain concept developed. Before their creation back in the thirties, drovers herded the livestock from the central regions to the coastal meat processing plants. But many heads were lost on the way, and it involved a lot of people.

Nowadays, farmers can send their stock along on a 'beef-train' whenever necessary. In this way, pricing and delivery routines became more streamlined and efficient.

There are truckers who specialize in livestock transportation. Beef cattle are driven in 'dogs' with two storeys, while sheep are packed in four-level carriers. These 'dogs' are sometimes as high as six meters and a fully loaded 'train' containing two of these weighs as much as 130 tonnes.

There's no denying that this method of transporting animals is not acceptable to animal lovers. Cattle that may have never seen a human being are driven and forced along by cowboys on motorcycles into large pens to await transportation to the coast. These cattle are wild since farms here are of gigantic proportions, the land stretching endlessly in all directions. The livestock fend for themselves on the open ranges. A farmer out here can be as far from as 500 km from his nearest neighbour!

A trucker's directions can cause confusion, since there aren't any road-signs in the outback. He might have been told to drive along a dried up river bed until he came to a farm about a 100 miles west of Birdsville. To miss that farm by a few miles is inexcusable!

When he finally gets there, he'll spend several hours eating, smoking, relaxing and talking with the farmer and his family, showering off the road-dust or just snoozing awhile in the shade before rumbling off again into the desert.

The loading up of livestock may be a disturbing experience. One sees terrified cattle bellowing and snorting with rolling eyes, tramping everything in their path, including each other. They are forced into the 'dogs' with whips and electric prods. As many as 130 are loaded up, but when loading sheep as many as 600 are packed in.

As soon as the driver has loaded, he has to make the distance, normally up to 2000 km, to the coastal meat plants in

under 30 hours. Temperatures will surely climb into the 40s Celcius. After about 35 hours the livestock begin to die both from the uncanny knowledge of impending death and from heat-stroke. That any survive at all is a miracle.

Out in the desert the dust gets so thick that the rig's cab is all you can see, the rest being swallowed up by the boiling dust clouds. Time is survival when transporting livestock, so speeds are generally about 90 to 100 km/h. One driver we talked to compared it all to 'hammering down straight for the gates of hell'! He concluded that at such 'flying' speeds you only hit every third pothole, which was good because at slower speeds you feel every hole and that would jolt and jerk any rig to bits, driver included!

That doesn't sound too pleasant, even though these rigs are 'plump'. Or what would you call a Kenworth 12-cylinder, 20-liters diesel, producing 430 horsepower with a 15-speed gearbox?

A standard type rig just wouldn't make it out here; too few gas stations, frankly. Or to tell the truth, none at all!

A rig operator has to play 'camel', hauling his fuel with him for the round trip. That normally means extra tanks holding round about 1500 to 2000 liters. Tyres present another special problem here, forcing every rig to carry eight spares on an ordinary run.

(Left) A roadtrain on an 'outback' desert trail. Lengths of up to 45 meters and weights of up to 150 tonnes seem sheer lunacy.

(Below) Drovers used to herd livestock through the desert with huge losses. Today roadtrains play an important role in Australia's cattle and sheep industry.

Over:

(Left) Room for only one. Not much left for a roadtrain driver to manoeuvre. When two roadtrains meet, the question is, who bites the dust?

(Right top) Three trailers, found only in 'outback' Australia. Weight and length limitations make them illegal in certain states.

(Right bottom) Coupling the trailers with the help of a crane.

To mention water is to talk about life; to lose a radiator hose because of flying gravel and rocks could mean trouble. Without·water you're finished. Truckers have died out here. Even if the water is boiling hot, it's a welcome sight as it bubbles from a tank.

These 'meanest of the mean' machines also come equipped with that Australian oddity, the kangaroobar. Made of tubular steel and mounted in front of the grille in order to sweep off the occassional kangaroo that bolts into the rig's lights.

There are 45 species of kangaroo out here, and they number in of the millions. Not to mention the freely grazing horses and cattle; a roadtrain driver who's up to cruising speed doesn't brake or swerve — it's a good thing they've got their 'roo-bars' as they call them. Barreling into a 90 kilogram kangaroo at 100 km/h can be a crushing experience...

Of course, the roo-bar is especially important for fibreglass cabs although some truckers have had unpleasant experiences when they forgot to lower the frame before tilting the cab hydraulically!

Back in the thirties and for awhile after, most rigs had double axles on the front as well as the rear. This gave better of

handling over the rugged surfaces. But with the appearance of powersteering, all that changed.

A lot of Australian rigs have air conditioning but there are still those who argue that nothing beats a hard breeze from a rolled-down window!

Of course, it's comfortable to have air-conditioning while it's over 40 degrees C outside, but if a trucker has to climb down into that blistering heat, he runs the risk of sudden sunstroke; if you're out there on your own, it could mean big trouble.

The Highway Department officials have been concerned over the fact that rigs are getting both heavier and longer. Where asphalt surfaces have been laid down, they've generally been ripped to pieces by the heavy loads, while macadamized roads have become nothing but holes on top of more holes!

The most trafficked route is the Stuart Highway, which runs from Darwin to Adelaide. The road is paved about half the distance.

For most parts, the route is only about 4.5 meters wide — in other words, room for only one rig at a time!

Roadtrains driving along the 'track'

AUSTRALIAN ROADTRAINS

stay on it, while cars wanting to pass have to take to the surrounding terrain in order to get around. If a rig should slip off the road and do the same, it would send boiling, choking dust high into the skies. There's not a windshield made that could withstand the hail of gravel and rocks thrown up by the churning wheels.

The trailers tend to sideslip and sway coming out of curves, so if they're empty they could be swinging quite a few metres off to the sides — any normally bright motorist wouldn't take chances by driving close to a roadtrain grappling through the desert!

The terrain itself is treacherous to both rigs and drivers. In some spots where the surface is worst, truckers have to sort of half-sit, half-stand up in order to save backs and kidneys from the beating. Many a head has been bashed and battered thanks to the catapulting effect of modern seats!

Since there aren't any viaducts out in the bush, roadtrains can easily attain their spectacular height. Bridges are pretty rare as well. Outback Australia is probably one of the few places in the world where they don't bother to build bridges, preferring to just let the road run straight through the streams! During periods of heavy rains, truckers often have to stop and walk along in the stream carefully searching for the tracks on foot before attempting to roll across. Every time they stop, they run the risk of getting remorsefully stuck out in the middle of the flash stream. Trucks have been known to be stuck in the muddy bed for several months before being towed out.

A refrigerator-trailer company had 16 rigs pulled up in the mud in different places at the same time, something of a record down here!

That same blinding, boiling, filmy dust that eats into every tiny crack and crevice, that clogs up many a fine engine, is the same gluey mass that sucks off your boots as you wade through it and that holds a rig fast up to its axles during the rainy season. Unless you've got a least a CAT D8 dozer for help, you can count on being stuck a long time!

Because of the combination of high speed, stress, poor visibility and non-existent road surfaces, wrecks and pile-ups are a fairly common occurence. Most of the time, rigs are so totally wrecked that they're left to rust silently in the desert.

Not just anybody has the makings of a roadtrain driver. It's not exactly your nine

to five job. Long hours under the worst possible conditions is the rule out here. A trucker has to be willing to work at any time and any place, under any condition. Most people probably couldn't handle the monotony of the ride; a good example is the trip between Darwin and Alice Springs or the 3300 km ride from Adelaide to Darwin... hauling extra tank trailers holding 70 000 liters on a modern rig with five axles and two five-axled trailers... .

Even though practically all cargo is hauled on these roadtrains you can drive sometimes for days and not see another soul, or another vehicle. All you see are kangaroos, hundreds upon hundreds...

The guys who manhandle rigs through this wilderness have a strange look in their eyes, can't handle crowded rooms, or everyday small talk. They even have trouble eating and drinking while on the road. In order to 'rehabilitate' them occasionally bigger trucking firms give them jobs in the terminals as depot workers to help them re-adjust to normal life!

It makes one wonder why these truckers carry on out here in the desert and the dust. Hundreds of miles of desert stretching away endlessly in all directions. Is it the money? Or is it the adventure?

This page and facing: Cattle are carefully 'packed' into the roadtrain. Then begins the 'rush' through the heat and distance. A delay usually means more heads lost. Roadtrains have taken over from the drovers in long distance livestock deliveries.

Over: The men behind the wheels of the roadtrains. Tough men working under tough conditions. Trucking here is no dream. Reality means a costant fight for survival.

AUSTRALIAN ROADTRAINS

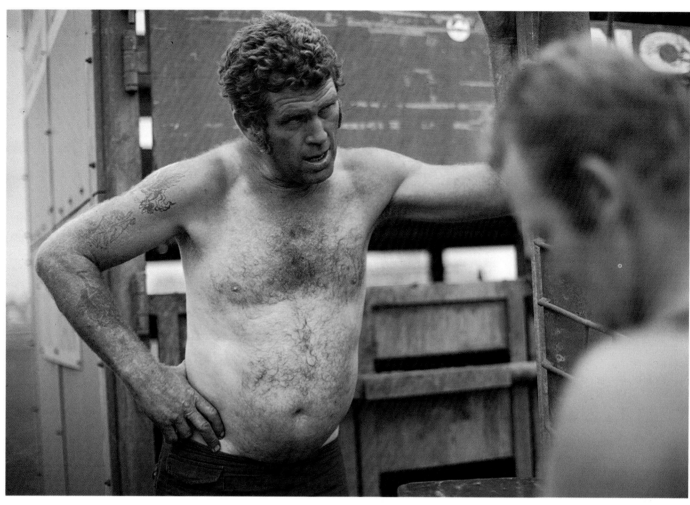

chapter 2

THE WILD ALASKAN

It was getting late and the day had lost some of its brilliance, but the light was still strong enough to put glitter on the blue-white Nelchina glacier. The mighty Wrangell and Chugach mountains rose up on the other side of the road and the valley beyond. It's beautiful and we could only savour the scene in silence as we sat by the window in the Eureka Lodge.

Behind us lay Anchorage and, according to the map, our next stop would be Glenhallen. If the sign standing proudly just outside the entrance could be believed, we were at the northernmost truckstop in North America.

We had our doubts. Just a few hours ago we were at Mexicana, another truckstop on the Glenn Highway, and a quick study of the map raised these doubts.

The question was whether or not Mexicana could hold that title instead?

But what difference did it really make?

'Of course it makes a difference!'

We should probably never have asked that question. Hal Fimpel, the owner of the Eureka Lodge, almost screamed and waved his arms around. He operates America's northernmost truckstop. And

nobody is going to question that, that's for sure!

'Mexicana lies on the south side of the road', he explained with red tinge on to his face, 'Eureka's on the north side. That makes us the northernmost. Or . . .?'

We sure didn't have any intention of continuing the argument. But we understood that we hadn't heard the last about Eureka Lodge. Hal Fimpel had already decided to give us the whole unabridged story.

But before Hal gets warmed to his tale, let's explain why we're sitting here at the Eureka Lodge, America's northernmost truckstop (we can't very well say its anything else . . .).

We'd planned our trip for a long time, and thought we'd ramble up the Alaskan Highway — or the Alcan Highway, as its actually called — from Anchorage to Mile 0 at Dawson Creek up in British Columbia. A nice little stretch of about 2500 kilometers, straight through the wildest, most rugged terrain you can imagine, the toughest country in all of North America.

We'd prepared ourselves as well as we could. As with a lot of other things in life, we realized that nothing around here is as it used to be, back in the 'good old days'. That expression feels right, somehow.

Twenty-five years ago, anything that rolled on wheels to Alaska was sent along the Alcan Highway. Today, the freight load is a ghost of what it used to be.

Ever since freight started being sent up along the inner passage from Seattle, by steamer and barge, trucking operations have had to give way. Today it is impossible for the trucking outfits to effectively compete with shipping on this route. But it isn't completely dead along the Alcan either; everyday, 35 rigs leave Anchorage.

And our trip was still an adventure, even in our modern times .

The Alaska Highway makes certain demands on a man. The trucking outfits long ago began signing contracts with one-man owner/operators. That's just about the only guarantee they have that the goods will in fact get to their destination, that the rigs will in fact roll.

Fred Christie, a veteran in the business, and boss of Lyndon Transport, gave us this explanation before we started out:

'If a guy drives one of my rigs, and gets stuck somewhere out in the middle of nowhere, you can rest assured that he will grab the first lift out of there. If I'm lucky, he'll call in by phone and let me know where the rig is standing. But, if he's driving his own rig, he'll get that thing running again no matter what the cost. He's sure as hell not going to leave his truck standing out there in the wilderness. The guys who drive for us take damned good care of their rigs, and they work like the devil, too!'

The Alaska Highway is no place for Sunday drivers . . .

We chose the spring as the best time for our trip. The Alaskan winter isn't exactly your idea of a holiday, let alone work. We knew that out there, were miles and miles of absolutely nothing and that the thermometer drops down to 50 degrees C below zero.

But even the spring has its pitfalls as Fred went on to tell us.

'Every season has its own problems. Right now, we've got the spring thaws to contend with. It causes a real hell for the boys. The roads are cracked and slick, and it isn't possible to drive faster than 50 kph. Not likely that anybody would be foolish enough to try either. Everybody knows that that's reasonable speed given the conditions out there. The trucker who follows the rules avoids a lot of trouble and headaches. Makes a little money besides. And that is what its all about, making a decent living, right?'

To drive along the Alaska Highway isn't just an adventure — it's a trauma as well. But, the guy who manages to keep his vehicle on the road, and is willing to work hard is bound to make good money. All the drivers up here manage around 15,000 kilometers per month. There are a few who manage to squeeze in 16,000 km or 17,000 km per month, but that's the absolute limit.

Hal Fimpel was starting to warm to his subject.

'Eureka is a truckstop', he said, 'Mexicana is just a place where hunters and sport fishermen stop off. We're a part of the National Truck Stop Association. We live off trucks and truckers. You can't make that claim about the Mexicana'.

We decide that it's reasonable to acknowledge Eureka as the northernmost truckstop in North America and Hal pounded us on the back happily.

We slowly rolled out from the lot at the Eureka. A little woozy from all of Hal's stories — couldn't tell you half of them — we let our eyes glide along the beautiful snow-clad mountains surrounding Eureka. We try to imagine what it must be like up here when winter has the area in its toughest grip.

We drove to the village of Glenhallen and on to a dirt road where we met a trucker whose rig was slowly crawling up a steep incline. We waved and he stopped.

Jean-Baptiste was a French-Canadian on his way to Emento, Alberta. He didn't have anything against a little chat.

He drives his own International, and told us that he'd just unloaded machine-parts in Anchorage and was running empty on the return-leg to Alberta. He didn't have a permit to load in Alaska. Usually he hauls machine parts up in Alberta.

'I generally take on a couple of hauls per year up the Alcan. Not because I make any money out of it, but because it's kind of like a vacation for me. There just isn't anything in the world as fantastic as this!'

'We're all unique.' Jean-Baptiste is a living example of that statement, because this idea of a vacation that he's got is a little different to say the least . . . We all agreed on that one after he told us about the storm he ran into during one of his 'vacation trips' on the Alcan.

'I parked out in the bush and it snowed for two days. There was only one thing to do: camp out in the cab. When it finally stopped snowing, the whole rig was completely covered by it.'

Over: The Alaskan or Alcan Highway is a stretch of about 2500 kilometers through the wildest, most rugged terrain.

THE WILD ALASKAN

We asked carefully if Jean-Baptiste ever felt afraid while he sat there in his ice-cold cab.

'Oh, no! I've been a fur-trapper and I could have made it through the whole damned winter out there! There were plenty of deer, so I wouldn't have starved. Well, anyway, when it finally stopped, I managed to get up on the highway and started walking towards Destruction Bay. After a while I met up with a police car completely jammed into a drift. When I got the boys out of there they were practically frozen stiff! So, as things turned out, it was me who saved them!'

We were on our way to Tok, which according to what we'd been told, lies at the junction between the Glenn and Alaska Highways. A real dump, we were told, or as one trucker in Anchorage described it:

'You're sure not going to like Tok. It isn't much to see, but all the same, Tok is there, out in the middle of nowhere!'

Rumoured it there's a truckstop in Tok.

Before we got there, we saw a girl riding on a horse. Just a little bit surprised, we stopped out in the middle of nowhere, miles from anything and anybody, to talk for a minute with Kelly Wilson. Besides her horses she had a dog, whose eyes made us think uncomfortably about wolves.

Kelly told us she was on her way to Winnipeg, a 5000 kilometer stretch. She'd camped her way along. Our first question seemed a little ridiculous. Wasn't she afraid of bears?

'I don't like bears', Kelly told us frankly. 'But as long as they leave me alone, I don't have any reason to make trouble with them. If they try any tricks, I'll just shoot them straight off.'

All we had to do was look into her eyes to understand how serious she was.

We finally arrived in Tok at about nine o'clock at night. There's still a bit of daylight left, but dusk is rapidly falling.

Between the Canadian border and Tok, there's a lot of nothing. Westwards towards Fairbanks it's the same.

A dozen or so houses set back from the highway looked for all the world as though they'd just been tossed there by some unseen mad hand. There's a police station, a weigh-station, two general stores, a garage, a souvenir shop with a tired and worn out stuffed moose standing outside the door with a saddle on its back, and then there's the Tok Lodge — the truckstop, of course.

Tok is surrounded on all sides by forests, but a fine sand is spread around outside the houses, and the gritty dust finds its way down one's throat and nostrils. It's an awful place, and you get the feeling that nobody would live here if they could avoid it.

We wandered into the bar at the Tok Lodge, which also functions as a reception desk. We asked for a couple of rooms for the night.

The man behind the bar reacted in an unexpected way. With a surprised look he tossed a couple of keys at us and demanded 30 dollars in advance. Maybe he was the owner. Maybe he wasn't. We didn't bother to ask.

We tossed our luggage in our rooms and strolled down to the restaurant. We'd been behind the wheel for a long tiring day, and our stomachs demanded a decent meal.

We got served a couple of giant, raw, and tasteless steaks. We had the sense not to complain. Tok Junction, Alaska is a long way from the promised land.

Art James, 45 years old, has driven a rig for 15 years, the last five in Alaska. Art's mad as hell.

He'd just driven up the Alcan from the 'lower 48'. That's what Alaskans call the rest of the United States when they're feeling especially disrespectful.

It was his first time on the route. After passing the border between Canada and the USA at Yukon, he was upset to say the least.

'All the way up through Canada, it's as clean and neat as you please, just like it must have been when the first white man came up to Alaska. The campsites are neat and tidy. You can't even find an empty cigarette pack on the roadside. Everybody respects the law about littering. But then, as soon as you cross that border into Alaska, the empty beer cans are everywhere!'

Art took a deep swallow from his glass. His jaw muscles tightened and his gaze hardened.

'Campsites look like pigsties. Car wrecks up and down the road. It all looks like one damned gigantic garbage dump! It's a damned shame! One of the most beautiful places on this earth, and we're turning it into a junkyard. We have got to keep this country clean, otherwise we just don't deserve to live here!'

A drunken Indian wandered into the restaurant, bumped into Art's table and spilt his beer.

The Indian, who was about Art's age

looked at him, and we saw by his embarass-
ed expression that he was ashamed. But he
was too drunk to manage an apology.

We were expecting Art's anger to boil
over completely, but instead he just looks
at the Indian with a sad, friendly
expression.

'That's alright, Jim.'

The Indian swayed, nodded his head,
and stumbled out again.

'It's not his fault', Art sighed. 'We
took everything they had away from them,
just left them the air to breathe. All we ever
gave them was bad whisky and misery.'

We really liked Art. He's tough, but
fair. He cares about his country and his
people.

From Tok, Alaska, up to Whitehorse
in Yukon it's about 650 kilometers. Even
though there are three towns marked out
on the map — Beaver Creek, Destruction
Bay, and Haines Junction — there aren't
enough people living up there to fill an
ordinary bus!

We were right in the middle of the
country that we were told was mile after
mile of absolutely nothing. But that's
quite right. We had already seen seven

moose, a few deer, a herd of sheep, two
bears, and five trucks.

We crossed the border between the
United States and Canada, and passed
into the Kluane Wilderness, which is
surely one of the most beatiful, if most
isolated, places up north.

We drove mile after mile along the
shores of the pea-green Lake Kluane,
formed by glaciers, while the St. Elias
Mountains rose up like a gigantic white
ghost to the South. This stretch contains
some of the highest mountains in North
America as well as the biggest ice fields
south of the Artic Circle.

When we arrived at Haines Junction,
where the road branches off to the south
towards Haines in Alaska and northeast
towards Whitehorse, we stopped off beside a rig parked at a hamburger-stand.

We ordered up some coffee and started
a conversation with the trucker. He's on a
scheduled route between Fairbanks and
Haines.

We had read that hundreds of eagles
fly down to Haines a couple of times each
year and asked him if they were there now

Over:

*(Left) A stop to fix a
blown tyre. Most manage
it on their own but when
the winter cold bites
down, drivers take
extreme care to make
good preparations.*

*(Right top) Drivers at the
Eureka Lodge. The
'northernmost' truckstop
on the north American
continent.*

*(Right bottom) A Ken-
worth on the Alcan
Highway.*

**THE WILD
ALASKAN**

Kelly Wilson. A lonely pilgrim in the middle of nowhere.

past, from the hectic goldrush days.

The next morning we wandered out to the outskirts of town to have a look at the Huskie, the town's only truckstop.

It was early in the morning and the sun had begun gliding over the beautiful ridges, rowing a pale gleam along the streets of the town. Two rigs were parked at the Huskie, and it didn't take long before breakfast was standing on the table, and we were in a lively chat with the two truckers, Al Simmons and Gordon Koppang.

Huskie is a little place, spartanly furnished, with just six tables. We were served by a young girl, no more than 11 or 12 years old. She's the owner's daughter and generally runs the place.

Gordon Koppang was on his way to Dawson City, but he had time to relax for a minute.

'The worst thing about this job has been a damned crane, 35 tons deadweight, which we've had to haul back and forth. I'll bet even you were in on this job', he said and turned to Al, who was just shovelling scrambled eggs into his mouth as fast as he could.

'I think every trucker in Whitehorse has helped out with that damned crane at least once', Al answered with a wide grin.

'Anyway, we hated that damned crane. Then, when a trucker was hauling it to Haines, it happened. He braked too hard at a sharp curve, and his trailer started sliding. It hit the side of the roadbed and that crane just shot off 30 meters into the air and landed in the bush! Like a rocket!

'He managed to hold his rig on the road, but that crane was smashed to bits when it hit the ground. Sure it was an accident, but I'll tell you, all of us were tickled pink when we heard about it! We even took up a collection for the trucker who'd managed to pull it off!'

'Not that he needed the money. His rig didn't take any damage, and he didn't get a scratch. We just thought he'd really done a good thing and we wanted to show our appreciation! That crane was just a pile of metal junk and it took four trucks to haul it out of there in pieces!'

Another trucker came into the restaurant. He grabbed a chair and sat down with us at our table. His name was George, and he laughed heartily when he heard the tail-end of Gordon's story.

'That crane was sent from hell, no doubt about it! Still, it didn't compare with those loads of meat . . . .'

by any chance. He laughed and said with a relief:

'No, thank God!'

Oh?

'Well . . . I hit one of those bastards last fall. It died right off, and I have never had so much trouble in all my life since that accident. I came close to getting two years in prison and losing my permit forever. But what can you expect? That damned fool bird flew right into my windshield, but they didn't give a damn about that. Those eagles up in Haines are so protected and coddled that if they screech at you, you don't dare yell back!'

Two days later, we were up in Whitehorse, Yukon Territory, Canada. Whitehorse has had two 'golden ages' in its history — the first during the great goldrush back in 1898-99.

When the rush ended the town shrank, and shrank. If it hadn't been for the railroad from Skagway, Whitehorse probably would have disappeared from the map. The railroad kept the town alive until the Alaska Highway was built in 1942.

Now Whitehorse has 15,000 inhabitants and is surrounded by untouched wilderness.

We slept the aches out of our tired bodies at the Klondike Hotel. Just the name of the place made us feel a whisper from the

THE WILD ALASKAN

'Yeah, right!' Al said. 'Tell the boys about that one!'

All three of them burst out laughing.

'Meat is about the worst thing there is,' George said, 'those carcasses swing back and forth, and that means real trouble in the curves.'

The boys at the table gulped their coffee and were all ears, even though they'd probably heard this story a hundred times before.

Something about good stories. They just get better every time you hear them!

George's adventure happened during May about two years ago. He was supposed to haul a load of meat from Haines. When he got up on a hillcrest it all happened at once. It was right after the spring thaws and the gravel road was loose and shaky.

'I got a little too far out on the edge, and even though I wasn't driving fast, it was enough to pitch me off the road. The rig turned over and the trailer got so chewed up that some of the meat spilled out.'

George came out of the crash without any broken bones. The only thing he could do was start walking.

'Haines Junction was about 30 kilometers from there, and I knew my chances of meeting someone were small. I made it into Haines about ten o'clock that night, and that was too late to get anything done, so I just had to wait until next morning.'

When the sun rose, George managed to scrape up a few guys and a trailer. The main thing was to save that meat, if at all possible.

'Well, when we came around that curve I got the shock of my life. Bears! Bears everywhere! There must have been at least a dozen of them, and at least two were grizzlies. The rest of them were black bears. You know, they'd dragged those carcasses all over the damn road! Some of them were dragging meat off into the woods with them! We sat there for half an hour and watched those bears having the party of their lives. They didn't even give us a glance!'

George had to return empty-handed. He finally got his trailer back up on the road several days later.

'There wasn't so much as a shred of meat left in that rig. Not enough even to make a plate of Irish stew!'

George and his buddies were bent double with laughter.

We realized that the boys were starting to get into high gear, so in order that the

'Mile O' Alaska Highway. More than 1500 miles to the other end.

tale-telling wouldn't take all day, we cautiously steered the subject over to the dangers of driving across the ice-covered lakes, something that is common up here.

We asked if anybody ever went though the ice.

'Why, sure,' George answered.

He took off his cap, and we all saw a long white scar running from the top of his head down to his left ear.

'I broke through, and got half my scalp taken off! Froze my right foot and almost got frost-bite'.

That was a few years ago. George was driving up with some mining equipment to a mine not far from the Dalton Highway up in northern Yukon.

'We usually drove across the lake,' George told us. 'A couple of rigs had crossed before us. I came driving down the slope and drove nice and easy out onto the lake. You have to be really careful so you don't make the ice start bouncing up and down. I'd gotten about a few hundred meters out, I guess, when all of sudden I heard a loud crash. The rig started tilting slowly over, and I realized I'd broken through.

'I felt that ice-cold water hit me and from that minute on I don't remember a thing. Somehow I must have gotten myself out of there because when they found me

Over: Companions to truckers. A pet husky, a wild bison and the trusted rig.

THE WILD ALASKAN

I was practically a mile from the spot where it happened. I was crawling on my hands and knees . . . . '

We asked George if he still liked being a trucker. He answered quickly and with no hesitation.

'Of course I do! I like my job, and it happens once awhile that I have to break the ice on a few lakes. I don't mind. I don't worry about it anymore. If you've gone under once, the chances of it happening again are pretty small. At least that's how I see it.'

We thought about the woman we'd heard about, the one who always carried a bomb in her purse when she flew. She figured that the chances of there being two bombs on the same plane were minimal . . . something like one in ten million.

We didn't bother to voice the comparison. We understood that George wasn't kidding anymore.

Gordon Koppang, who had been sitting sipping his coffee while he listened to George's story, cleared his throat and looked at us.

'You've got to understand, there's just nothing like driving up here in the North. There's just something about this old Alcan Highway that gets stuck in your blood. I love this road. I've driven down south, on freeways and in cities, but I don't call that driving. The Alaska Highway is different.

'Maybe you think these long stretches between towns and urbanized areas feel lonesome, boring? You're wrong there. In some unexplanable way, this road is more alive than any six-lane highway you'd care to name.'

Complaints aren't something the truckers along the Alaska Highway are known for, that's something we'd learned from our travels up here so far.

THE WILD ALASKAN

Every single soul seems to love it.

We rolled out of Whitehorse and left the Huskie truckstop behind us. Our last stop was Dawson Creek, British Columbia, up at Mile 0 on the Alaska Highway.

During this monotonous trip, somehow the wild and savage wilderness had left us indifferent, we realised that not a single police car had shown itself during the entire ride. We remember what Fred Christie, boss of the Lyndon Transport Company let slip while talking to us just before we started our long journey.

'Our biggest problem is axle-weight', he'd said, 'but at Lyndon, we weigh every load that leaves the terminal.'

'Well . . .', Fred muttered and leaned back in his chair. 'Sure, it happens that we catch a little trouble now and again. But the truth of it is that there aren't too many patrols between Anchorage and Fairbanks. You see, there's just one trooper to patrol that whole stretch!'

During our journey, that one policeman had other work to do apparently.

It was Sunday morning when we finally rolled into Mc Dermonts truckstop in Dawson Creek, and there was a rig parked by the entrance to the café.

It didn't matter, we told ourselves. This was our last and final stop on this job. End of the line.

All we really cared about right now was a giant, hot, steaming breakfast!

McDermont's truckstop is bigger and more modern than most of the ones we'd seen during our trip. We ordered some ham and eggs and asked to speak to the owner.

A good-looking waitress told us he was in church.

So we decided to forget about the job and enjoy our breakfast for a change. We talked over our experiences, and noticed that three old boys at the next table were listening curiously to our conversation.

It wasn't too long before we found out that they were all truckers.

Buck Whiteford asked if we'd stopped at May's Kitchen close to the top of Pink Mountain. We explained that we'd missed that one.

'Too bad, she's got the best food, and the biggest servings in all of Alaska!'

Buck has driven the Alaska Highway for 15 years.

'Back in the good old days, there were more truckstops and cafés, so when I drive up and down now, I feel sad to see all those places closed, all those people gone, moved away. Makes you feel more lonely than ever before', he said.

Buck's two buddies, Art Lyste and Gordon Malkinson told us some wonderful stories about life out on the roads, and Sunday morning moved away into the afternoon.

We heard about how Buck spun round with his rig and almost broke his back, how Art saved some American tourists from certain death from the cold, and was offered a fat wad of dollars and turned it down.

We don't have room for all of their stories, but let's just listen to Gordon for a minute:

'It was in the dead of winter, and I had just come through a curve and on to a straight stretch. I saw a car coming towards me at high speed. All of a sudden it swerved and headed for my radiator. I threw the rig over as far towards the shoulder as I dared, but I was sure that this was a certain head-on collision. At the very last minute the car swerved and disappeared over the edge at the other side of the road!

'When I managed to stop the rig, I ran back, prepared to see the worst. I found the car upside down about 75 meters down a steep incline.

'All smashed up. Then I saw four youngsters slowly crawling out of the wreck. Not one of them had gotten so much as a scratch!

'Well, I was happy that no one had gotten hurt. But I was really shaken, myself! I felt that old adrenalin pumping and I grabbed the closest boy, and yelled 'My God, boy, I thought you were going to run right into me!

'He looked at me with a silly expression on his face and said with a surprised tone, 'Aw, hell, I had the situation completely under control!'

Laughter echoed and bounced off the walls of the café.

Over: A lonely Peterbilt. It's not just an adventure. It's a trauma as well. But the guy who manages to keep his vehicle on the road and is willing to work hard, is bound to make good money.

THE WILD ALASKAN

chapter 3

ICE-COLD NORWAY

In Norway the truck is essential. Stretching 1752 km in length as the crow flies, this country is 430 km at its widest, and just 6 km at its narrowest point. The unbroken coastline is 2650 km, but taken at its full length it's a fantastic 22,500 km long, or the equivalent of halfway around the world!

Norway's brand of coastline, broken and jagged, can't be found anywhere else in Europe. The fjords, carrying the North Sea deep into the interior between cliff-like mountain-sides, gives the landscape its characteristically rugged beauty. These fjords, coupled with endless mountain ranges, make railway development an impossibility.

'Linjegods' is Norway's largest domestic hauler and was known until 1973 as 'Godscentralen' — 50 per cent of which was owned by just one man. Today, 50 per cent of the corporate stock is controlled by a holding company consisting of several independent truckers. The remaining 50 per cent interest in held by the Norwegian State Railroads (NSB).

The existing railway stations are being phased out by NSB. These stations, scattered throughout the countryside, are being taken over by Linjegods and turned into trucking depots.

Freight forwarding is carried out with trucks run by stockholding members. The only way in for an outside trucker is through direct purchase of a member. An exception is made for local distribution, where light trucks and vans are sub-contracted.

In Oslo there are several depots. One of these is Alnabru, where we met Eivin Gunnarson.

'Out of a total of 1400 employees, 200 work out of Alnabru, and all of us drive a truck', he told us. We also found out through Eivin that just in the Oslo area, 75 light trucks are in use for local distribution, while at least 100 tractor-trailer units are rolling per day on scheduled routes.

One of the longer routes runs between Oslo and Hammerfest. That's a 2200 kilometer trip. But to get there, carriers have to roll first through Sweden, then through northern Finland, and finally back into Norway again.

'As you can see', Eivin said with a smile, 'Our domestic traffic is a little unusual'. The choice of route shed some light on the geographic difficulties facing a carrier.

Since the terrain is what it is, truckers often utilize ferries in order to save miles.

'In addition', Eivin added, 'we're

building up a transportation system with containers in conjunction with NSB. As far as possible, containers are moved by rail to selected terminals where they are reloaded onto flatbed trailers or ships. We are committed to creating a cheaper, faster, and safer freight forwarding system'.

Such efforts are of course a threat to the trucking industry in the long run, but the terrain will always give the Norwegian trucker an advantage in their battle against the railways, than say their colleagues on the continent.

'Linjegods isn't the largest freight forwarding organization in Norway, even through we sold transport services for 635 million Norwegian kronor in 1979; Eivin said, 'but through our co-operation with NSB, we believe we will be within a few years. The struggle for market shares is a question of cost and quality'.

There are many freight-lines in Norway and starting a new organization is difficult. The State exercises control over the market.

'The Department of Transport has complete insight into the different freighting organizations and their market profile. Anyone wishing to start on his own has to apply for a special license. Thanks to that, there isn't any risk of an overcrowded field; on the surface this might seem to obstruct free-enterprise, but the system does keep existing forwarders solvent, and truckers rolling; Eivin said.

What's really like driving a tractor-trailer in Norway? We decided on a 600 km ride with a rig bound for Molloy, the most westward point in Norway. Our driver was Ragnvald Nygaard, who drives a Volvo F89 tractor-trailer, which at 18 meters, is the longest vehicle to be found on Norwegian roads.

We started out about four in the afternoon, planning to arrive around nine the next morning.

As far up as Kvam the trip was relatively quiet. But still, the E6 past Hamar, Lillehammer, and Ringebu can't be compared to some other European highways!

We got off the E6 and turned into Highway 15. 'You can catch some more sleep; he said after a while, 'and I'll wake

This page and over: The roads in the wilderness are idyllic during summer. But when winter comes, they become the toughest places to work in.

you when it starts to get interesting. We woke an hour later. How far to Stryn? Ragnvald glanced at his watch, 'About two and a half hours'. Distance isn't measure here in kilometers, it's measured in time!

'The farmers are already up and about,' said Ragnvald, and we no longer felt so alone. The time was 4:30 am. The road was crooked, but still paved. The soft rumbling of the Volvo became gradually more high-pitched, almost complaining, so Ragnvald down-shifted and said, 'Now we're going up Scandinavia's highest mountain, Galdhopiggen, 2469 meters high!'

We had an hour's crawl at 20 kilometers per hour ahead of us. It was the Alps all over again! The asphalt gave way to gravel and the road became narrow and twisting, with small streams crossed by stone bridges. The cabin shook from the engine's vibrations. Hard on the nerves, and hell on the ears, but for a trucker like Ragnvald, just part of the job. He'd driven this route for the past ten years, and before that, had manhandled a bus along the same route, for the same company, NS, or Nordfjord & Sandmore as they are known in Norway.

We hadn't seen a house, car, or any other sign of life for the last hour. But, right at the top stood a fantastic, super-modern restaurant . . . closed, of course! A roadsign pointed off to the left towards Stryn. Ragnvald just blasted on by. Hey, weren't we going to swing off here?

'No, that's the old road,' Ragnvald explained, 'just wide enough for one rig to crawl through on its tracks, and so twisted it tied knots around itself! Usually it's closed during the winter months, and the people living over that way are shut off from the outside world until the spring. For as long as possible, the Highway Department kept the road open with plows and snow-clearing equipment, piling up snow along the road higher than the truck! At several places the snowbanks were widened so that traffic could get past.

'Once though I met another trucker, but was I lucky! I only had to back up about a kilometer before we could get past each other. But it has happened that two rigs have collided, and had to be left in the mountains until the spring thaw!'

'Now we're going to drive through that damned mountain that I used to have to crawl over, and that made me three hours later getting home,' Ragnvald growled. We drove through the mountain two more times.

'These are the famous three tunnels that are known to every Norwegian trucker', Ragnvald told us as we came out into a valley. It was like meeting a new world; the jagged and broken crags above the tree-line were replaced by lush greenery. During the winter the tunnels are closed during the night, since the Highway Department doesn't think it economically feasible to keep the tunnels open 24 hours a day. Because of the weather, the tunnels have to be constantly swept clean of drifting snow at their mouths.

We still had quite a few kilometers to go before we reached Stryn. The road narrowed again, and crawled past several lakes right up against the mountainface. Ragnvald pointed off towards the mountain. 'See that? That's from the avalanche we had here last spring! Took a week to clear the road! One could plainly see where a piece of the mountain's side had been washed down by last year's spring thaw.

At 7:30 am Ragnvald was home. He lived in Lindset, just a few kilometers outside Stryn. There, perched on the mountainside is his villa which he built with his own hands.

About an hour later we heard the hoarse cry of the Volvo's horn. Time to say goodbye to Ragnvald, and get going. Another trucker was going to run us the last 80 kilometers to Molloy.

The trucker really fills a function along this route. We stopped everywhere, at country stores along the way. It was two sacks of cement here, a few cartons of staple goods there, and even a couple of sacks of potatoes at one stop!

Our new driver manhandles a bus from Molloy to Stryn in the mornings and wrestles a tractor-trailer back in the evenings. He is used to it all and didn't find it strange.

'But of course, in the winter it can be downright troublesome, since the water running off the mountains freezes into crystal clear sheets of ice on the road. Driving 40 or 50 kilometers through that causes some special problems!'

But stop driving? Not on your life! That never occured to him. The freight has to get through! What would the people of the Westland do without these truckers and their rigs?

ICE-COLD NORWAY

chapter 4

A BRAZILIAN EXPERIENCE

We were prepared, but nevertheless amazed by the proportions. Brazil is the fourth largest nation in the world.

But then figures are, after all, just figures.

3116 kilometers in a truck gives you a different perspective.

But let's start with some facts.

Brazil is a republic with 22 states, four territories and a federal district — Brasilia.

The country is spread over 8.5 million square kilometers and has a population of 120 million.

The largest trucking company, Di Gregorio Distribuicao e Planificacao de Transportes Ltda, has 1300 employees, 250 vehicles and 5 ferries.

Impressive even on paper!

We came to Brazil in order to scout a transport operation utilizing both ferry and road networks. Setting off from Sao Paulo in the south, trekking northwards 3116 km by truck to Belem and 1713 km by ferry along the Amazon River to Manaus nestled in the Amazon jungle.

4829 km through six of Brazil's 22 states!

Things went wrong right from the start.

We were going to take a premier ride in the first Scania R 142 model to be manufactured in Brazil. The rig was delivered on a Friday — our take-off was set for the following Monday — the R 142 had purred smoothly from the Scania plant to Di Gregorio.

But when Monday came, it wouldn't budge an inch.

Amazement, embarrassment and panic. Knowing smiles here and there were mixed with the suggestion that we put in a new pump.

Franco, a son of the powerful owner, Agostinho Di Gregorio, asked:

'Did you have it tanked up in town?'

Yes indeed, the Scania had in fact been tanked up there, which gave the immediate answer to our problem, since the fuel available on the street is unclean.

The tanks were pumped out and refilled. The Scania started easily.

We might have a trip after all!

But what awaited us? Fast tongues had already painted a frightful picture;

Tales of bandits, battles with jaguars, snakes, crocodiles and insects were shrugged off.

However, the prospect of poor roads and inhuman comforts had us more worried. Unrepaired roads and impossible overtaking conditions were disturbing facts.

Not to mention the Sao Paulo traffic.

Sao Paulo deserves a mention as it's one of the largest cities in the world.

Nobody's quite sure whether there are 8, 12 or maybe even 15 million people living here.

At any rate, here you will find more than one and a half million vehicles and more than 30,000 factories.

Every day 15 to 20 Di Gregorio trucks leave Sao Paulo for Belem.

By the time we were out of the terminal, 16 other rigs had already left. Right into the middle of rush-hour traffic. We looked on admiringly as our 'motorista' (as drivers are called in Portuguese), José Gianesini, extracted us from the city. He gave a real lesson in 'chaos-escape' tactics! Paraguayan born José, one of the pioneers on this route got our respects from the very first.

Also along with us was Paulo Albino Bernardes, the first driver to be hired by Di Gregorio. Nowadays he carries the title 'fiscal' (inspector) and his work entails inspecting service centers, motels and restaurants along the road network as well as drivers and vehicles.

A Chevrolet station-wagon tagged along just behind us. We knew it was there just for our sake. Because in it sat Mario Lima, director of Saab-Scania Brazil's PR office.

José decided not to take the shortest way out of Sao Paulo — instead he took a longer, but less trafficked route which lead through Itatiba, where we got back onto the 'right road'.

After about 20 kilometers we reached Campinas and stopped for a quick shot of coffee. And raised some eyebrows.

Nobody had seen the new Scania. The spoilers attracted a crowd of 'carreteiros' (Portuguese for truckers). Everybody wanted a look under the hood.

What's the size of the engine?

388 horses, ready for work.

José checked the tyres and listened to the engine.

'She's not turning over right when standing', he said. 'If it's not, maybe it won't be smooth at higher speeds either.'

We climbed back in and with the taste of hot, sweet coffee on our tongues we rolled back onto the road and passed by the truckers from the motel.

We passed rigs one by one on the steep inclines; the small, often heavily loaded trucks practically stood still.

We realized in a hurry that the Brazilian plateau is anything but flat. Sometimes it's up to six kilometers uphill, with grades between eight to ten degrees sometimes even more! It's slow, very slow indeed.

But downhill, anything goes.

Irregardless of the steep inclines, the narrow lanes and the intense traffic flow, most carreteiros blast along at top speeds. The familiar smell of scorched brake-linings lingers at every curve.

Straight stretches are covered at incredible speeds. Overtaking? It makes no difference whether you're on a hill or twisting round a curve; and driving on the wrong side of the road.

'You have to, when there's something blocking your lane.'

'Heart in mouth', literally.

On the freeway just outside Sao Paulo, a heavy-equipment trailer had gotten 'hung up', blocking half the road.'

That didn't seem to bother anybody though. The quickest way around the obstruction was the other side of the road — with flashing lights and screaming horns. Traffic rules only exist in theory.

Generally speaking, one just drives wherever there's room.

There is one thing that Brazilian carreteiros stand by. Once they've decided to pass, that's it. Out on the lane, there's no changing one's mind. No matter what.

A dead carreteiro is a dead carreteiro.

A cross is set up over one's trucking buddy, that's about it.

We saw a lot of crosses along the roads.

As night began to fall, we arrived at Ribeirao. We'd had our daily dose of thunderstorms; for an hour it poured while the sky continuously flashed and snarled.

More or less blinded by this natural force, we stumbled into the hotel, congratulating ourselves for having successfully covered 300 of the 3116 kilometers we'd set before ourselves. Three more days to Belem.

It became clear to us that we'd have to break some records the rest of the route! All the same, the next day José decided we had to take time out and check the pump. He wasn't satisfied with the way it was working. Another day more.

390 kilometers out of Sao Paulo . . . the freeway ended and before we entered the world of harrowingly narrow roads we expressed our disappointment at not having met any 'treminhaos' (tractor-trailer combination that's up to 28 meters in length and 83 tonnes gross weight and used for sugar cane transportation).

A BRAZILIAN EXPERIENCE

However, we were about a month too late to see any of these seasonal rigs!

Instead we shoved off into the fruit district. Every hill had us as tense as piano wires, you never knew if there'd be one, two or even three vehicles abreast shooting over the crest to meet you! Outside Uberaba we stopped at the Cinquentao Motel on 'Big 50' (That's the local name for Rodovia BR 050 — BR means 'Federal Road').

Once again, the R 142 pulled in a crowd of curious on lookers. We walked around and stretched our legs while we saw the most amazing cases of overloading possible. On a three-axled open platform Mercedes 1513, for example, one carreteiro loaded up 19.8 tonnes of lumber. Perhaps he confused the rig's weight of 19.5 tonnes with it's maximum load specifications?

After we'd passed Uberaba, our 'fiscal' Paulo wanted to stop at a motel where several Di Gregorio vehicles were parked. Their drivers looked slightly embarrassed when Paulo asked them if they'd stopped for the food or the overly-friendly girls.

José moved on out with the Scania bound for Uberlandia, where we'd agreed to meet. José'd have that pump taken care of there once and for all.

Paulo offered us a ride in the 'tank' to Brasilia.

As we glided down the BR 040, Paulo told us a little about himself. We find out that he's married and has six children ages 7 to 29 years.

He talked a bit about just how much a rig means to its owner; how the Brazilian truckers lover their rigs like a part of their family. That's why most rigs, even older models, are well-kept and spotless. Paulo thinks that the route between Sao Paulo and Belem is a real vacation. Nowadays the trip takes about 96 hours — before, it took four weeks!

Along the BR 040 we see many people walking, as they seem to do everywhere in Brazil. Women and children out looking for a river to wash clothes in. Families with sacks and bags searching for the bare necessities; food, water, wood, utensils and clothes. For most of them, the local garbage dump is the only place where one can look.

Even though Brazil is one of the countries with the most buses you get the feeling that the normal means of transport is feet, or a flatbed trailer.

Dogs and pigs wander in and out of the villages freely, apparently nobody cares about them.

The scarsely clothed, hungry and dirty children is a depressing sight. We saw them everywhere, begging or peddling.

Pretty soon we were to meet the contrast. Brasilia. A city without slums, an orgy of architectural 'firsts'. An unseemly monument surrounded on the fringes by trash houses. There the slums are total.

Brasilia is a newly built city out in the middle of nowhere. All freight is hauled to and from the city by road. That road is easy to describe: hills, hills and more hills. Overloaded 'oldies' piloted by proud but wildly gambling carreteiros fill these roads in all directions.

Most of the rigs are Mercedes-Benz 1113s, Fords, Dodges, Chevrolets, Fiats and Volkswagens, three-axled units with long flatbeds.

Brasilia was officially opened in 1960 and practically ruined the nation economically. It was meant to be a city without slums.

All the same, just outside Brasilia the slums spreaded like wildfire. That wasn't supposed to happen — but it did!

At first glance, it's hard to understand just what the politicians were thinking about. There must have been so many other things to invest the money in.

The road to Anapolis is as hilly as the one from Uberlandia. In places, the old trucks crawl along at barely ten kilometers per hour. The many Merc 1113's practically stood still!

Beside the exit ramp for Annapolis, a group of 'chapas' sat under a tree, waiting for trucks that might need help with loading and unloading.

A day's work brings a chapa between 2000 to 3000 cruzeiros. For exceptional loads, up to 5000 cruzeiros.

The job opportunities are sporadic. It can sometimes be days between jobs.

When we met up with José again, he held up both hands in a characteristic 'thumbs-up', while his face shined happily.

'Now she runs perfectly!'

In Anapolis, the new Brasilia-Belem road begins, with several 'test' stretches where different road coverings were tried out. Everywhere we looked we saw highway department workers.

Suddenly at a low spot in the road everything grounded to a dead stop. A Fiat and trailer had crashed. The wrecks stood dumbly at the spot where it happened — in the middle of the road!

Several carreteiros, impatient to be on

A BRAZILIAN EXPERIENCE

their way, geared up and crawled around the Fiat along the shaky edge of the road. Their rigs wobbled wildly from side to side, but nobody tipped over.

Later, we ran into a downward stretch. It must have been ten kilometers long. Along this stretch, many carreteiros drive 'banguela'. Which means that they disengage the gears and roll her all the way down . . . the road's reasonably straight, and there's nothing in the way, so why bother to brake? That ride goes fast, really fast.

Overloaded rigs are more the rule than the exception. Broken springs is a common ailment. These roads are rough. But most of the blame must be put on overloading.

There are plenty of weigh-stations, but we didn't see many carreteiros outside them. More stations are planned, and more and more are being opened along the road net work.

'Only dummies actually stop!' José told us. The signs set the speed limit at 40, and stopping is supposedly obligatory for all trucks.

The people working at the weigh stations don't even look up as the rigs go by.

'They wouldn't react even if we blasted the horns at 110 km/h!' . . . he went on.

We met several rigs loaded on top of one another. It's a common way to save fuel. We even ran into a rig hauling a trailer with a trailer on top of it, and on top of that, a tractor!

'It's a good way to make money', José told us. 'The boys split the money they make out of it. The owner pays for fuel as if they'd both driven themselves.'

According to José, livestock and vegetable hauliers are feared the most out on the roads.

'They drive like madmen, the vegetable mustn't rot, and the livestock mustn't lose too much weight'. He explained.

It seems as though all of Brazil has been invaded by Mercedes-Benz 1113s! They must have sold hundreds of thousands of them down here. We rummaged through our notes and came up with some figures relative to the trucking in-

The ride through Brazil's beautiful terrain runs along broken and bumpy roads. For an outsider the different routes seem to take a lot out of a man.

Over:

(Top) Vegetable Express is the most feared. Two truckers team up to take on stretches for 40 straight hours without rest.

(Left bottom) You can see some fine rigs, even in Brazil. This is an unusually well-kept Fiat.

(Right bottom) Hills, hills, and more hills. All the same those truckers hammer right down. Pushing the rig to the absolute limit, and taking a big chance passing slower traffic on the crests of hills.

A BRAZILIAN EXPERIENCE

dustry in Brazil. There are in all 100,000 trucks of less than 10 tons load capacity, 500,000 with payloads of 10 to 20 tons. All the Mercs we'd seen are in that class. In the 20 to 30 ton class there are about 75,000 vehicles, while there are 60,000 registered for more than a 30-ton load weight.

In the heaviest class one finds mainly Scania, Fiat, Mercedes and Volvo. The Scania taking us on our long journey to Belem is one of the heaviest; it's an R 142MA 4×2 tractor with a 3.8 meter wheelbase. Behind us we'd got the three-axled covered trailer put out by FNV-Fruehauf, the most commonly used trailer in Brazil, and according to Franco di Gregorio, the best on the market down here.

The Scania is of course, a real luxury when compared to the average rig rolling down the Brazilian roads. All the same, the farther north we got, the tougher it became to take care of everyday comforts. We had to take care of our needs out in the bush.

It was during one of our obligatory stops that we ran into our first Brazilian snake. Thank God it was a dead one! The pale skin on its underbelly stretched a good 15 cm wide, a sizeable monster. Swarms of ants were over the carcass, and we saw that the snake had just gobbled up a spider as big as a crab, before being pulverized by some truck's wheels.

We had two days and 1600 kilometers ahead of us before we reached Belem. Perhaps now was the time for us to meet some of the bandits and 'highway men' described to us in such detail!

We passed a burnt up rig. All that was left was the roof and chassis.

We'd be seeing many scenes like this one up ahead according to José. Flats and dividers are often constructed from wood, so with the Brazilian braking technique and their poor tyres, a burning brakelining or a smoking tyre often lead to greater troubles!

Pretty soon we came up to a burnt-out hulk of tanker. She must have gone up like a bomb!

'They're all bombs', José sighed.

A heavily loaded Mercedes 1113 struggled with screaming engine up a steep incline, and José eased in slowly some distance behind it. We gratefully realized that he wasn't planning to roar past before we reached the crest! The Merc had four yellow lights out back, identifying it as the most dangerous thing on the Brazilian road — a vegetable express.

'They hammer down from Sao Paulo to Belem non-stop', José declared. 'It only takes them 40 hours or so. Fruit and vegetables on the way up, rubber and melons back down. Always fast, so the load won't spoil!'

Two drivers work the route tandem-style, and according to José, drugs and alchohol are the only means to keep awake. The rigs have such small cabs that the guy trying to sleep has to curl up like a ball, either in the passenger seat or on the floor!

'It's really crazy. Last trip I met one of those that had driven off the road. Both of them died.' He went on.

When we stopped a little later at a small motel for a steaming, syrup-sweet cup of coffee, we met a man who was living evidence to what José had told us. He had just collected the belongings of his 19 year old brother-in-law. The guy had driven a little Merc and met up with a 'vegetable express' at the crest of a hill while passing.

One more cross for the roadside.

Temperatures hold pretty steadily around 30 degrees C, and it got hotter the farther north we drove.

'It's raining over there!' José pointed towards the horizon. It soon felt cooler.

Unfortunately, with the rains comes humidity. From 80 to 85 percent, which is the norm around here, up to over 150 percent! We were sitting in a sauna!

We rolled by a big road repair job. Some men with shovels were leaning against some light trucks. No signs, no warning flashers. The only protection they'd taken were big rocks they'd rolled out onto the road.

Reflectors are an unknown entity in Brazil. It is a miracle that there aren't more crosses than there are!

We spent the night in Gurupi, at the Transbrasilianas Motel.

After scaring the roaches half to death and chasing out the lizards, we slept like angels.

The heat hit us worst on the fourth day. At seven o'clock in the morning it's already 30 degrees.

We had 1400 kilometers to go.

North of Gurupi the road stretches in a 120 kilometer long straight line. This is where a lot of carreteiros make up for lost time. It's hammer down and no brakes, for all they're worth!

In Barreteiro, a village like many we'd passed, José and Paulo took us to a restaurant, Boom Prato.

Christina runs the place.

A BRAZILIAN EXPERIENCE

It's a simple place, but clean and neat. From loudspeakers, the strains of 'Je t'aime' flowed smoothly.

The service was overwhelming, efficient and fast.

Well, we'd gotten the picture already. Boom Prato doesn't make its living from great coffee and cakes.

Boom Prato is a whorehouse.

'Find one in every village', Paulo told us

José and Paulo started bragging about their new rig, and of course all the ladies just had to see it at any price.

It passed inspection. The beds were popular.

At Fatima, the road narrowed, and got worse; potholes on potholes and bad patch jobs. José told us that it was here, just outside of Fatima, that a 'vegetable express' rammed a De Gregorio rig. All three truckers were killed.

Paulo placed the crosses over his buddies' graves.

In a little village we drove past a place that looked really fancy and carried the name 'Belem-Brasilia Palace Hotel'. We muttered about stopping, but our minds were quickly changed.

'You can't stop here', Paulo told us as he jerked his thumb down.

' Nothing but trigger-happy cowboys here. The whole village is trigger-happy. You don't stop in this town for a flat tyre, even. Better to limp out of town and fix it on the other side.' He went on.

The next village got the same recommendation.

'The ladies here are more beautiful and willing than ever', said Paulo. 'So nice that it's off-limits to all of us who work for Di Gregorio. If any of our boys stop here, they're fired right away'.

'It used to be impossible to get the boys up in their rigs and rolling again. The few times they managed to drag themselves away, they ended up burning rubber and brakes, costing money needlessly, as well as getting themselves killed trying to make up lost time'.

So now all the Di Gregorio rigs cruise through the town, but not without envious glances at all the rigs standing around there.

We'd reached the forested regions of the state of Goiá, with its gigantic sawmills.

We crossed Transamazonica, the talked about east-west route through Brazil — the road that never got finished. The deserted road just stands there with its unfinished stretches successively being reclaimed by the fast-growing jungle.

A little farther north, at the Tocantins River, we passed the border between Goiás and Maranháo. As at all state borders, we had our papers checked by the Posto Fiscal.

We bedded down in Imperatriz, a town of more than 100,000 inhabitants. It used to be just a small village before the road was paved back in 1947. Now it's the hub of the forest industry.

The place looked like a Hollywood film set for a cowboy movie!

Before we dozed off at one of the flea-bitten hotels, José and Paulo talked a little about their working conditions.

Di Gregorio's drivers get in about 120,000 to 150,000 kilometers per year. That amounts to two or three trips a month.

Their pay is around 60,000 cruzeiros per month, which is good pay in Brazil. No other truckers get as much.

Normal working hours are from four in the morning until ten at night. Everyone is entitled to a few hours siesta during the hottest hours of the day.

According to the law, it's legal to work for 12 hours per day. Every fourth day a trucker has to rest for 24 hours. That's why Di Gregorios drivers are off for one day in Belem before returning home.

When they reach Sao Paulo, they've got 48 hours off before taking on their next load.

Over:

(Left top) Modern technology hasn't completely taken over. You can still see an occasional load being drawn by horses!

(Left bottom) When two drivers team up, they try to keep the rig rolling non-stop. One drives while the other sleeps.

(Right top) Nothing beats a break out in the open country, where one can eat food brought along for the trip and prepared by the roadside.

(Right bottom) The Brazilian truckers often take on complicated repairs right by the side of the road.

Meals out under the open skies. This trucker and his wife prepare all their food themselves. It's cheaper that way.

55

A BRAZILIAN EXPERIENCE

The tax-rate is 10 per cent, and an additional 8 per cent is withdrawn for welfare costs. As an employee, a trucker has 360 workdays per year. Two days off at Christmas as well as two days off at Easter. Nobody works on the national holiday.

Those employed by Di Gregorio are entitled to a yearly vacation, which is something their colleagues don't have.

Speed limits are 80 km/h and apply to all vehicles in Brazil. Maximum load weight, without a special permit, is 45 tonnes with an appropriate number of axles and horsepower, of course. Axle-pressure is set at five tonnes for front axles, ten for single rear axle, 17 for bogies, and 25 tonnes for triple bogies. Maximum length is 18 meters. 'Treminhaos' up in the sugar cane districts are given special permits for up to 83 tonnes and 28 meters in length.

To establish oneself as an independent trucker in Brazil isn't hard. Through banks and credit institutions, one can borrow 70 to 80 per cent of the cost for a maximum of 24 months. Through leasing companies up to 100 per cent can be borrowed for up to 36 months, and through the State-run credit institution, Finame, loans are given for Brazilian-made rigs 50 per cent of the cost for up to 36 months.

However, it's expensive to borrow money. After awhile, one doesn't know exactly how large the debt is. Devaluations keep coming one on top of the other. In just ten months during 1981, Brazil devalued their currency by 88.8 per cent! Diesel prices went up at the same time by 110 per cent.

Freight rates, which are set by the government, don't go up at the same dizzying rate, however.

We fixed a flat the next morning and headed north once again on the last leg of our trip, through jungles and bandit-infested roads.

In Acailandia the 'new' Brasilia-Belem road ends.

We met up with three-axled Mercs hauling lumber and some small two-axled Dodges and Fords. In a curve we came across a Scania 111 with its trailer lying beside it.

The driver said he'd fallen asleep at the wheel, He was unharmed and had hung up a hammock in the cab in order to finally get some much needed rest!

We are confronted by our last Posto Fiscal at the border between maranháo and Pará. Just across the border we rolled through the vast black pepper plantations. The bushes looked more like coffee-plants!

It started to get hilly again. On one of the roadsigns we read: 'Check your brakes'.

Paulo had us stop for a minute before we headed up into the hills. He wanted to show us a forest of crosses — they'd been raised in memory of killed trucking buddies and relatives. We counted 35. Paulo said that 26 of these crosses were raised after one single accident — between a bus and a 'vegetable express'.

We were in no man's land. Not a house, not a human to turn to should anything go wrong.

For truckers out here there is only one rule: convoy. Di Gregorio's drivers aren't allowed to drive in anything less than three rig convoys in this area.

At night they aren't allowed to drive at all.

The road is narrow and the undergrowth reaches the roadbed in many places. The hills are so steep that the rigs barely crawl along at walking pace. This is the ideal spot for highway robbery. It's a simple matter to jump up onto a running-board with a knife or pistol ready and make the driver stop.

The load disappears quickly. Usually the rig is found, with the driver bound hand and feet. Sometimes beaten to death or shot.

It happens far too often.

Another well-practiced method uses two vehicles. One drives up ahead of the victim while another closes in behind. Then it's an easy matter to force the trucker to a secluded spot where another rig waits to be reloaded with the victim's freight. In the best scenarios both trucker and rig are allowed to drive off after the operation is completed.

We made it through no man's land without incidents, and in Ipixuna we met up with several carreteiros who had strung hammocks between some trees and their rigs, or under the flatbed of their trailers. It was siesta time and the trucks had been driven in under the trees in order to get some shade.

We changed over to highway BR 316 at

There are many hills in Brazil. Tough slopes that sap the strength out of both man and machine.

Over: 80 km/h is the maximum speed allowed on the Brazilian motorways. But, anybody who isn't absolutely honest, who doesn't follow the letter of the law, soon forgets all about rules and regulations.

A BRAZILIAN EXPERIENCE

Santa Maria do Pará and only 120 kilometers more to Belem.

Temperatures were hitting 35 degrees C, and sweat was pouring down our shirts!

José knows the road like the back of his hand — all the same, he made a mistake. The road ran downhill, with a dip and a bridge below us. Just ahead of the Scania there was a car. A piece of the bridge roadbed caused the car to swerve wildly, and José just managed to warn us before we were bounced around a lot worse than if we'd been on wild horses or rodeo bulls!

Before we'd collected ourselves and realised what had happened, it was time for another bump. Not a bit less wild than the last one.

A miracle that the Scania stayed glued together. That the cab didn't break off from the chassis would always be a mystery! But a point to José's cool nerves. Otherwise we might not have driven away from that one!

Belem is a big port at the mouth of the Amazon. It has 1.3 million inhabitants, and at least a million mango trees — some of them as tall as five storey houses! Mangoes come raining out of the trees like bombs, and when it rains and storms, the people of Belem look up when they walk around!

Belem was the end of the line for us, as it was for José and Paulo. For José, it's just a matter of driving down to the harbour and switching trailers, getting his documents at the office, and then 24 hours of blissful rest before returning to Sao Paulo.

Paulo was going to seek out some of Di Gregorio's other rigs and do an inspection of them.

We found out from Di Gregorio's branch office manager that the storms we'd been skirting had washed away two bridges. Those rigs ready for the return leg had two alternatives — the trip would be close to 4000 kilometers now.

We had our problems, too. Our timetable wasn't holding up, so we'd missed out on a ferry-ride to Manaus. Just to get a feel of the conditions, we managed to hitch a ride on one of the tugboats in Belem's harbour.

The ferries consist of a barge that carries 15 trailers and a 'pusher' — a tugboat pushing the load from behind. We were on the 'America', whose Captain told us that the trip up-river goes at about seven to eight knots. Down-river it's faster, about 12 knots. It takes about 115 hours to Manaus, while it only takes about 72 hours in the opposite direction.

'America' and her sister ships are driven by two 11-liter Scania diesels. During one round-trip sailing, the 'America' uses up almost 17,000 liters of fuel.

The crew consists of seven men.

Di Gregorio aren't the only one's to load trailers onto ferries — a lot of companies are in competition with them.

(Right) In order to avoid being smashed from the rear, it pays to be as visible as possible; so why not a sign to attract attention?

Of course there are rules regarding maximum load weight, but they are seldom taken seriously; the chances of getting caught are minimal.

It costs about 210,000 cruzeiros to haul a tractor-trailer combination roundtrip. The trailer alone costs around 160,000 cruzeiros.

Where there aren't any roads. Air freight is the only alternative.

Manaus is a freeport, so its expansion has been enormous. The electronics industry especially, has grown explosively during the last few years.

Being declared a freeport and therefore Free Trade Zone has been a lifesaver for Manaus.

Development has been explosive, not least regarding transportation. Big plans are being made here for the future as well.

However, far off on the horizon, the clouds are gathering. The fast development rate has meant that the rolling stock of the large trucking operations have had to be replaced all pretty much at the same time. That means big costs and with an eye to the merciless rate of inflation, coupled with the constant devaluations, it would seem that all economic calculations would become outdated very quickly.

The cost of fuel, tyres, spare parts, service and salaries increases more or less daily.

Brazil is a nation with fantastic potential. The country's resources are often improperly used.

We had seen some of the problems here during our trip. We had managed to slip through the bandits, snakes, crocodiles and jaguars. To our relief! We were worried at times though.

Principles aren't something to be ignored, that's true. But they can become a little worrisome when you're ready to follow them to the grave.

Over:

(Left top) A 'carreteiro,' which means trucker in Portugese, seems to regard traffic laws and rules with a cavalier attitude — it's all a question of getting the freight to its destination on time, there's no time to pay attention to 'strange' rules.

(Left bottom) Brazilian truckers love their rigs and take care of them well. Often they mean as much to a trucker down here as does his family.

(Right) 'Chapas' is the name down here for terminal personnel who help truckers load and unload.

A BRAZILIAN EXPERIENCE

chapter 5

TRUCKING FESTIVALS

The heat in the tent was insufferable; Linda, six years old, heaved a sigh of disappointment when the gentle bear 'Big Dez', withdrew from the tent.

She couldn't see what we saw — how the 'gentle bear' dragged off his mask and gulped down a pint of beer just outside.

The bear let out a satisfied burp and declared: 'What a carnival!'

We didn't hear the rest of what the bear had to say, because up in the sky over the tent, two madmen were going through the most fantastic air acrobatics.

The Marlboro Aerobatic Displays drowned out all our words and thoughts in a tremendous crescendo of screaming engines. Festival. Carnival.

This is a Trucking show!

We were in Peterborough, more exactly at the East of England Showground, but it could just as easily be Odense in Denmark, Mantorp in Sweden, or Le Mans in France.

Somebody mentioned that close to 80,000 people are at the festival. Truckfest '84 was breaking all records!

We sure didn't have any reason to doubt the figures.

Maybe it was like this during the era of horses and wagons . . . .

Shows, business deals, a lively party.

As we criss-crossed in and around the different truck fleets: Ford, Leyland, ERF, DAF, Scania, Volvo, and Mercedes-Benz; inhaled the smell of hot dogs, popcorn, hamburgers, bought a pizza from a rebuilt double-decker, or top it all off with a donut, the comparison seems valid!

Horses have been exchanged for machines, that's all.

Otherwise, the difference isn't all that great.

Ben Lester, the clown, was performing with his car. The bands were playing. A giant hot air balloon was slowly rising into the sky.

Both the police and the military were there, a kennel club was parading its dogs and in the middle of it all TV stars were arriving by helicopter, receiving the applause and excitement of the crowd. BBC Radio personality Sheila Tracey, was welcoming the celebrities to the tunes of a marching band. It was a real live 'folkfest' — fun and packed!

The chopper rose gently from the ground and in a few seconds the panoramic scene was spread out before us. It's an impressive sight.

No doubt about it. The days of the

(Right) The trucking 'culture', with its highly customized rigs is appreciated by a lot of people. Not least the young.

Over:
The festival is the place where people from the whole industry gather. Here you'll find music bands, truckers, manufacturers and 'common' people.

TRUCKING FESTIVALS

(Above) Trucking festivals provide family entertainment. The rigs are admired by many people.

(Right) It's natural to take the family along to the festivals be it in the UK, USA or continental Europe.

TRUCKING FESTIVALS

Horse trading fairs and markets have returned — in a new shape, a new atmosphere.

Everything comes into being because there exists a need for it. Trucking festivals are no exception.

Truckfest '84 was living evidence of what it can be like when market forces are given an opportunity to steer developments.

The trucking industry has a real need to meet with associates, and share experiences, not the least with those people out there who drive the rigs down the endless stretches of highway! Because in the long run, it's their viewpoint that counts, the one that tells it the way it really is. The traditional market atmosphere is evidently the right way to do it. High up in the air, we could clearly see the results.

Trucks, trucks, trucks and more trucks! Inside exhibits and outside exhibits. All sizes with all kinds of superstructures. Standard makes and models straight off the production line.

(Above) The show trucks are subjected to the scrutineering eyes of photographers and visitors. Just like the horse-trading fairs of the old days.

(Left) The colorful lacquers are so enticing that you can't help but reach out and feel them.

Over: Something that causes quite a flutter to weak hearts. The giant engine roars and shoots a flaming spout to the awe of onlookers.

TRUCKING FESTIVALS

(Above) The crowd can be pressing.

(Right) The moment of truth has arrived ... contests of various types are arranged at the festivals. Ranging from best looking truck to contests in economical driving. The excitement and tension are high every time a winner collects his prize.

(Far right) The motifs painted on the rigs are usually highly detailed. It has become a means for unknown artists to make their way in the world, to spread their art among a wide public.

TRUCKING FESTIVALS

Finely lacquered customized rigs from trailer manufacturers. Never before have so many truckers and members of the trucking industry gathered together at one time, at one place in Britain.

We saw queues everywhere, for every attraction. Queues to the catering tents. We tried to imagine how many cubic meters of beer would flow down those thristy throats before it was all over? The tank-trucks are running non-stop back and forth.

At the same time, we heard the critics in our minds. There are critics. Lots of them.

The normal reaction when stirrings of the first Trucking festival flow though a nation. The trade is afraid that the serious aspects of the industry, the real business dealings will be swallowed up by the tingle-tangle, carnival-atmosphere, and the hamburgers.

But those voices usually die away pretty quickly once things get started — Truckfest '84 was no exception.

It's the second year in a row that England has experienced a Trucking festival. Those critical voices from the previous

TRUCKING FESTIVALS

year had not deterred the organizers. The day was a success. There can be no doubt — Trucking festivals are here to stay!

So far, only the 24 hour Le Mans, in France can present larger gate-figures.

The industry has accepted Truckfests. Everybody knows that the arrangement is a success. Exhibition space reservations for next year have already been placed — most of the trade want to be sure they will have larger exhibits next year.

The rigs, which rolled in from every corner of England, had their cabs jam-packed. Families and relatives. Not to mention neighbours. When the rigs have discharged their human cargo, and there's only the trucker left, polishing away with his rag, the fun begins!

The kids lined up for ice cream. Grandma and grandad browsed through the stalls, while others made a beeline for the beer tent. The visitors aren't just truckers and their families, however. People from all walks of life show up at these events, the curious, the fun-seeking. Truckfest '84 has attracted people from all over Peterborough to the East of England Showground. They come to see for their own eyes the marvellous machines that make up a truckers everyday life. Maybe some even come to see one or two 'beasts' that frighten them out on the highways.

Trucks have always been thought of as big, cumbersome, slow-moving monsters that mostly just seem to get in the way.

The confrontations turn out to be pretty tame. Those frightful truckers are ordinary men and women, just as family minded as the next person. And those 'monsters' turn out to be good-looking

machines when seen close up! In effect, well-kept equipment and actual places of work.

Just maybe some people have realized that without those 'juggernauts' pounding down the asphalt day in and day out, there probably wouldn't be any food on the table, nothing to drink — we couldn't even clothe ourselves! Without the truck the ordinary goods of everyday living would simply cease to exist. All that which we take for granted would suddenly become crucial in their absence.

As we touched down with the chopper, we were right in the middle of an intense judging session! You see, a Truckfest isn't just a showcase for the truck and the people who live and work around it, it is also a contest, with prizes and glory! The contests included at the Truckfest '84 were

many: Best Kept Truck, Best Custom Truck, Best Vintage Truck, and Best Fleet Entry.

Prize money and Trucking International magazine trophies are given to the three best entrys in each class.

An additional prize goes to the Best Trade Stand.

The judging is serious. Twelve experienced members of the trade inspect vehicles and present an appraisal of the standard of safety and upkeep of each one. Their protocol is given to the actual jurors, consisting of seven men, all of whom hold key positions in the industry. These jurors inspect the vehicles once more before the finalists are selected.

To the sound of blasting sirens, hooting horns and roaring engines, prizes and kisses were awarded generously, by

(Above) Trucking festivals are also places where a wide variety of tradesmen from the entire industry present their products and services. New products are introduced, deals are made. Festivals engage people, motivate them and create an enthusiastic atmosphere.

(Opposite) The guy who wins a prize wins a lot of attention as well. Which is part of the payment received for the hard work and the labour of putting together a fine rig.

TRUCKING FESTIVALS

(Above) A real rig doesn't just have a well-lacquered cab. Even the trailer gets a going over.

Previous spread:

(Left top) Good looks aren't everything. The rigs have to be effective as well, if there's going to be a living made!

(Left bottom) Trucking has created many 'heroes'. Ex-prizewinners who've become known for their rigs.

(Right top) Companies don't waste any time getting the message out at the festivals. Through sponsoring well-known figures they get an excellent opportunity to expose their products as well.

(Right bottom) Since they are such special constructions the jet-trucks and their drivers attract special kind of attention and interest.

TRUCKING FESTIVALS

popular Sheila Tracey, of course!

The contests at the various festivals foster friendly competition and mutual understanding among truckers — and is a breeding ground for trucking favourites and legends! Trucking festivals create 'heroes' who become either loved or hated. 'Heroes' are those whose rigs have been found to be exceptionally effective or startlingly well-designed and/or customized. The rig becomes a model from which others evolve while at the same time symbolising the professionalism of trucking and truckers.

Manufacturers are, of course, quick to take advantage of the sudden exposure given by the media to these 'heroes' of the festivals.

Eric Bergen, of Denmark, unknown by his real name, but already a legend as 'Mr. President', was quickly signed on by Bandag, and travels all over Europe in a Mack, cruising from festival to festival.

Another trucker who got his name up in lights is Hans 'Mr. Trucker' Delsing, with his Iveco sponsored 'Jewel'. The rig is of course an Iveco Magirus.

From Sweden, Svempa Bergendahl, winner of innumerable prizes and awards, is backed by Scania.

Many others are strung out behind these 'stars' plugging for their success.

Alec Hicks had just gulped down a beer in the hot tent where Linda sat waiting for that nice gentle bear to come back.

Alec was responsible for the Shell Diesel Drivers Club, and a tent had been provided for curious members — 32,000 of them at the moment — who would be showing up for the festival. Together with 'Little Lizzie', the club's secretary, and the bear 'Big Dez', of course, he was trying to handle the load!

'We raised our membership by 500 the first day', Alec told us with a mile-wide grin, 'Before the year's out we'll be up around 50,000!'

Alec Hicks is convinced that there is a real meaning behind the trucking festival idea.

'These get-togethers mean an lot for the industry as a whole', he said, 'not just for the manufacturers, but for tyre, parts, and equipment dealers as well.'

Alec went on to claim that the truckers get more and more of a say in their own working conditions, their own living terms as regards choice of vehicle and equipment, thanks to these meets.

'Just tell me a better way to get out there and show truckers what there is to offer', he dared.

The heavy crowds to and from the Shell Diesel Drivers Club hadn't only been due to the good reputation of the club — no, 'Big Dez' had been doing his share as well! Not to mention 'Little Lizzie'. One trucker took such a liking to her that he just had to show her to his dog.

Another guy invited her to New Zealand.

If she's not back next year, who knows? Maybe she accepted the invitation.

However, Shell wasn't the only truckers club at the festival. Al Truchers Club, South West Truckers Club, Diesel City Truckers Club, and Truckers International Association (TIA) were all represented.

TIA had even brought along a trailer jam-packed with club items all the way from Sweden to Peterborough!

Especially sharp was the Leyland T 45 Team, who had prepared a special courtesy lounge for their members. Kay Mac-Dowell, T 45 Team's First Lady, offered beer all around.

When the sun began to go down over the East of England Showground in Peterborough, and the public filtered home, the remains proved that this has been a festival.

Everywhere we heard praise for the successful arrangements. The critics were silent now.

'This has been carried out in a fine way', says Dermot Bambridge, PR Manager of Scania GB.

'Of course, I have a long list of proposals for improvements, but I'm already looking forward to the next Truckfest!'

'We couldn't have dreamed of a greater success', we were told by Mike Thomson of Petercare. 'The introduction of Ebro got an enormous response, so you can bet we'll be back next year!'

We did our level best to find someone who could at least say something negative just for the record. We couldn't find anybody.

But then, somewhere out there on the roads, somebody is sitting and swearing over Truckfest '84. Probably swears every time he hears the word 'truck'.

What the heck, that's human, and easy to shake off. You can't convert a nation overnight. Or can you?

(Above) One of the most advanced contests is the manouevring test, in which the machines tiptoe in and around the cones in a manner not thought possible for such giants.

Over: The parallel between trucking and cowboys who crossed the wilds of the old West is obvious. Not least from some of the motifs on the sides of the rigs.

TRUCKING FESTIVALS

chapter 6

CALIFORNIA INSPECTION

Truck inspection and weighing station, 2.5 miles. Many a truckers' hands have begun to sweat when confronted by this sign over the years. A little more than four kilometers from Thousand Oaks, the sign hangs by the three-lane Ventura Freeway, Highway 101 north of San Fransisco just outside Los Angeles county.

We saw the next sign a few minutes later: ALL HEAVY TRUCKS IN RIGHT LANE. At the sight of this sign many big bakelite steering wheels must have become slippery with the perspiration of nervous truckers. Pall Mall cigarettes would have been lighted and smoked eagerly. Striped flanell shirts would get sticky and hoarse voices begin to sing along with the country music from the radio, but maybe the wrong song or the wrong tempo.

If the California Highway Patrol wants to check your rig there's just no way to get out of it! Sure, you can take another highway north, but it will take hours longer and it'll probably be your last trip for that particular customer. 'You're out of business, man!' In other words: just follow the signs!

Then you'll have to drive into one of California's seven weighing stations, strategically placed on the most heavily trafficked highways, at State borders and outside the big cities. It's the police's own little drive-in chain!

The visit won't slow you down more than a few minutes either. Actually you can keep your Freightliner or Kenworth rolling practically the whole time. If you're driving in the clear then all you have to do is gear up and roll out on to the Ventura Freeway again. However, if you've got anything you'd rather hide then just about anything can happen. It could cost you a small fortune in fines or you could be stuck there with a driving ban on your rig, or in the worst case, you could end up with a lot of both!

And don't waste your breath trying to talk your way out of it, the California Highway Patrol have unlimited piles of traffic tickets and they couldn't care less if you've got 13 kids and your job depends on your delivering your load on time. Forget it. They'd far rather see you out of a job than risk their own. The moral of the story is: life goes on, as long as you're clean with the California Highway cops!

These stations not only check weights and log books, they also inspect the equipment to make sure the trucks are in proper running order. You pass over the scales slowly and then drive into a building where a man checks the number of axles. If you're not overweight you get a green light which is attached to a post further along. This means that the Highway Patrol wishes you a pleasant journey. The green light is the most common occurrence but there is also a red light — then you're in trouble!

You'll get a red light if the checker behind the glass partition has calculated that you're overweight or if he decides that your rig needs an overall inspection. There is a loudspeaker on the same post as the light and through this, the checker will tell you how to proceed.

And you'd better do what he tells you!

We moseyed into Robbie Robinsson, the man behind the glass. He's an elderly man and sits dipping cookies into his coffee mug.

Huge trucks rolled past the window the whole time: Kenworths, Peterbilts, Freightliners, Macks, Internationals. Most of them are well decorated of course, with candy-colored designs, neat painted signs and chrome, chrome, chrome! Sometimes they pass at a few minutes intervals and sometimes with practically no interval at all.

Robbie is incredible. As he sits sucking on his coffee-dipped cookies he calculates the fluctuating digital numbers that show the weights in pounds. He figures in his head!

'Uh, if you've worked for the Patrol for 12 years then you get used to it and you notice quick if a *fat one* crosses the scales', he said modestly and popped a cookie into his mouth. Robbie once had his own truck workshop so he knows the industry from the inside.

He told us that during two shifts, from 8 am to 10 pm between 1000 and 1500 trucks pass over the scales.

'The rush hour starts at eight in the morning and lasts a couple of hours, when the working day begins for the drivers coming from Los Angeles in the south. On the other side of the highway it's just the opposite, the busy period is in the evening', Robbie explained as he munched on his cookies. He meant, of course, the other half of the station at Thousand Oaks, on the opposite side of the freeway. It takes care of the southbound traffic, excess weight and the sweaty hands.

There is a second digital meter on

Robbie's table that shows fluctuating numbers even though there isn't a truck around on this occasion. It wobbles between seven and nine and the scale is a cryptic KC/M. The numbers are counted X 10.

'That measures the radioactivity. It shows now the amount in the sunlight and air particles (slurppp!) and that's usually what you see', Robbie said.

Many of the trucks haul plutonium or uranium and they check that here too. Of course, there are very few leaks. It's happened to Robbie once.

'The meter flashed up and showed 200 so the guy had to park and phone for service', Robbie said. Actually 200 is not really dangerous, but it's enough to turn on the red light. The limit is 100 on the meter.

Robbie considered that it was far worse when a guy showed up 15 tonnes overweight. The truck was unloaded and given a hefty fine.

And there it was, a red light! A real good-looking Freightliner came to a stop and Robbie reached for his microphone. The mike was surrounded by cookie

The inspection station officials are all highly qualified, most of them are ex-mechanics with excellent merits. They can almost 'hear' if there's something wrong with a rig.

Over: The Thousand Oaks inspection station is one of California's seven strategically placed stations along the most trafficked routes.

CALIFORNIA INSPECTION

crumbs and through it the driver learnt that it was 'inspection time'. Robbie checked and added up the axle weights. He checked to see that nothing was hanging loose from the truck and trailer and assessed whether or not it was inspection time. The inspection stickers are stuck on the lower left-hand corner of the windshield.

'Turn around, inspection time, lane 2!' Robbie shouted, and we wandered over to California Highway Patrol's lane 2 to have a look.

Inspection goes quickly too. Men in overalls converge on the truck and inspect all the brakes, fuel and other lines, couplings and all other equipment that has to do with safety. During this time the driver can buy a cup of coffee, a Coke or a Mountain Dew from an automat, or he can go and take a leak.

The Thousand Oaks station is built into solid rock and the whole place echoed with the sound of air-powered wrenches all the while we were there! When the inspection is completed the driver is given a new sticker and may continue on his way. Now the inspectors themselves can take a leak. Then it's time for the next inspection.

We then met for the first time a guy who looked like a real policeman. Ray Wineinjer is his name and he came out of the office building and looked at us suspiciously. Private cars are not allowed to drive in here and a Saab Turbo is not much like a Kenworth. But when we explained what we were doing we gained a Highway Patrolman as a friend for life.

Ray told us everything we wanted to know and, among other things, that he owns a Porsche 914 and a '57 Chevy and that he always drives at 55 miles per hour. He told us that there are six police officers and nine inspectors working at Thousand Oaks station. The officers are dressed, like him, in uniforms and the inspectors wear overalls. Ray is the Commercial Enforcement Officer in charge and his buddy Bill Right holds the same position.

'The inspectors are all highly qualified and have all previously been first class truck mechanics. It's almost as though they can hear what's wrong with a truck even when it's stopped,' Ray laughed and invited us into the office.

The first thing we saw as we entered was a large display board with police photos of accidents in which trucks were involved. The photos don't only show smashed-up trucks, there are also pictures of smashed-up people!

'They have a deterrent effect', Bill said, and he couldn't be more right.

Their patrol car, a Dodge, is parked outside ready to take off anytime. If any foolish optimist tries to make his Peterbilt invisible and imagines he can pass the station unnoticed then the patrol car goes out and gets him. It happens, but not often.

'Yeah, if we're not too busy we catch the guy and give him a 65 dollar ticket. And if we suspect he's overweight or he is guilty of safety violations or due for inspection then we show him the way back', Ray said and explained that the major function of the station is inspections. There is a scale because it's handy to have in conjunction with inspections, but there are lots of separate weighing stations along the highways.

'The drivers all know we're here and so very few of them try to sneak by overweight or stuff like that', Ray said, and added that during an eight-hour shift there are only two or three overweights.

Most often the drivers aren't aware of it so Robbie, the cookie man, will usually allow them up to 100 kg overweight. Above that, the tickets come out and unloading is enforced.

Sometimes there's a wide variety of goods piled up within the area waiting to be loaded on an incoming truck that the violator has talked into helping him. And the goods had better be picked up before 10 pm, because then the station closes. But then all the violators can just smoke a cigar and drive with the hammer down, right?

'They can try! All members of the California Highway Patrol are trained on trucks and the regular patrols are just as scary', Bill said, and he has a CB radio close at hand, although shut off a lot of the time.

'Yeah, you can't listen to that thing, 'cause there's an endless babble on it.'

Ray then took out his revolver and showed us, taking it just as much for granted as he would his car.

'A Colt?' we asked, trying to show we knew the score: we'd seen Kojak and Baretta.

'Nope, it's a Smith & Wesson 357 Magnum. We had some problems with the Colt. They're not popular any more. A Smith & Wesson is a perfect hand gun, even if you don't use Magnum ammunition. I use 38s; they're terrific.'

'Yeah?'

We backed away from the office and headed for a parked Peterbilt that was being repaired. A rig, that is, that hadn't passed through the careful inspection check. Actually a careful check on this truck wasn't necessary. It was out of Oklahoma City, Oklahoma and was in bad shape when it rolled into the station a few hours earlier.

When a truck fails to pass the inspection then it is relegated to the parking lot and the driver has to see that it's repaired the best way he can. The Highway Patrol itself has no repair mechanics. The driver will then phone his boss, who usually knows a number of companies he can call. In this case Bob Dill had to drive his GMC service truck out to Thousand Oaks from Los Angeles.

'I have 450 regular customers who phone when they have troubles with their trucks, but I only handle tyres, brakes and springs.' Bob said and seemed a little stressed. He had his son along to help him on this particular job.

Bob shook his head as he examined the truck and said that soon some truckers will drive with any equipment at all just as long as it rolls, then he pointed out a few of the faults with this particular rig. There are quite a few!

All the air cushions in the truck's springs were flat! One spring blade was broken, the blade that supports the whole rig! On the trailer one of the pins that hold the axles in place had come loose and the axle had moved back, pinching the brake lines. No brakes!

The guy who drives the truck slept sweetly in the cab on a fat violation ticket, and it took Bob Dill exactly 25 minutes to fix everything! He moves like a demon between the truck and his complete Grumman tool kit.

'I've got everything here I need to fix anything: leaf springs, hoses, gas and electric welds, compressed air; you name it, we have it!' Bob said with professional pride. He also mentioned that Peterbilt trucks are a little more difficult than some others and take longer to fix. He's worked on every model there is.

Bob's company 'Truck Repair' has two GMC service trucks, one that handles tyre business and one for leasing and rental trucks.

'If you're fast, this job is a good deal', Bob said, and for this particular job he took 400 US dollars, including parts. He quickly gathered his gear together, got the driver's signature on the order and roared off to the next job. He tooted his horn as he passed the man behind the window and received a few crumbs of cookies via the loudspeaker on the post.

Robbie blinked the green light for us as we drove off onto the Ventura Freeway again. The truck traffic is intense, and it is an impressive feat that thousands of truckers follow the signs to the station and that this steady stream is kept moving. With only two to three overweight loads during an eight-hour shift, there are law-abiding drivers as far as the eye can see!

Opposite:

(Top) As long as you're clean, the inspection isn't a problem. However, if you've got something wrong with that load, then you've got trouble.

(Bottom) A rig rolls in for an inspection. At the Thousand Oaks inspection station, they look over between 1000 to 15,000 trucks every day!

Over:

(Top) The inspection-stations are the Police's own 'drive-ins'. Nobody gets through without having been thoroughly checked first.

(Left bottom) Some loads contain plutonium and/or uranium. The personnel at the stations have equipment to measure radioactivity.

(Right bottom) You can see a lot more than broken-down and overloaded rigs at the inspection stations. Here for example, a finely painted and cared for Peterbilt.

CALIFORNIA INSPECTION

chapter 7

AN AFRICAN ADVENTURE

The flies had wakened after the siesta, but the dogs were still sleeping heavily in the Tamanrasset heat.

Indoors it was beautifully cool. The beer is good and cold at the bar of the Lune Rouge. A few hours later the sun set over the Sahara and threw its dusky light over the red-toned buildings.

At sunset Tamanrasset is blindingly beautiful.

It was our second day in this Algerian centre just south of Hoggar, the impressive mountain massif. We were still tired, and none of us had so far any wish to continue the long journey to the sea. We were dozy from the leisurely atmosphere. While drinking our beer we listened absent-mindedly to the conversations going on around us at the bar.

'You can't get any help any longer out on the roads.'

The Australian gentleman's nose was red, and he'd probably paid a heavy price for his bottle of whisky.

'Shocking awful roads. We came across a couple of vehicles near Seouenout, both were completely stuck. They couldn't move a meter.'

'What was wrong?'

The bar tender couldn't resist asking.

'No idea.' The Australian emptied his glass.

'But they beckoned us over.'

We had already doubted a couple of times if we really were quite sane. The idea of leaving a safe and well-functioning Sweden for an uncertain and, to say the least, reckless future as drivers in a tiny African country was perhaps not especially well thought-out.

What did we know about Togo? Who knew anything at all about the area if it came to that? To the west is Ghana and to the east Benin. On the northern border is Upper Volta. To the south the Atlantic — Guinea Bay. A harbour town, a few lagoons, thick rain forests but for the most part barren savannahs.

It all began in Morocco.

Capricious customs officers had just shrugged their shoulders. Forbidden to drive trucks through Morocco! Only after endless discussions and the embassy's help were we able to reach the Algerian borders.

The first customs officer demanded a stamp that can only be obtained in Algeria. Permission to drive a private car in Algeria could possibly be gained from someone else.

After yet more calls to the embassy and a journey by bus, train and plane, we finally obtained the right stamp. After payment of the tidy little sum of nearly 300 pounds sterling, the Algerian roads lay open to our Mercedes 2232.

Well, 'roads' is perhaps an exaggeration. They're called 'ring fences', thoroughfares marked by sticks stuck in barrels. Heavy trucks and military desert vehicles destroyed the sandy surface a long time ago. And it will probably take several centuries before the rains, so rare in this part of the world, make the sand firm again.

The further out to the side of the thoroughfare you go the better. The unused sands give a better grip than the actual ring fence. But if you drive too far from the fence then you don't know if you're still following it. For the fence is not a straight line: it winds round sand dunes, rocks and wadis (dried up rain-water furrows).

We'd been warned. At certain spots the fence would be so badly marked that we could easily cross it without even knowing it. Should you find yourself on the western side but believe yourself to be on the eastern, you can easily end your journey in the middle of no man's land.

Only once were we near to losing the trailer. It got buried in the soft, treacherous sand. We were forced to release the trailer and use the tractor unit to get us to the nearest village. It took us two days to find the place again!

We'll never forget our first night in the Tamanrasset. Alex had kept us awake until the sun rose over the tops of the Hoggar mountains.

We could still be sitting there with our beers and Alex's reminiscences, since what Alex doesn't know about trucking in Africa isn't worth knowing.

Alex is one of the trucking pioneers of Africa.

'I was supposed to be driving building materials between Monrovia and Nimba,' Alex told us. 'Nothing special about the stretch — just 300 kilometers. There was just one small problem: they'd forgotten to tell me that there was no road'.

Alex had come to Liberia to drive trucks. But there weren't any roads. What do you do then?

'Well, you build a road'.

It seemed to be the most obvious thing in the world for Alex.

'There was also another little problem hanging over us. To reach Nimba we needed 242 bridges. 242 bloody bridges!'

There isn't much point in trying to keep the trucks clean. The heavy work soon ruins the best efforts!

Over:

(Left top) Roads in Africa are not for fancy driving. You have to gear your driving to the circumstances, which at most times, are very demanding.

(Left bottom) Roadworks in Africa required a lot of foreign expertise until a few years ago. Thats why so many Europeans came down here, to work and find adventure.

(Right) During the rainy season the bad roads become hopeless. But the freight has to get through all the same, which does create some problems.

AN AFRICAN ADVENTURE

Alex and his African colleagues set to and built them. The method was simple. They laid two palm tree trunks over the river bank, and between the trunks a plank.

'It either held or snapped', Alex sighed. 'Sometimes it held, but often it gave way'.

People often forget the difficult, unpleasant things in life. They are inclined instead to remember only the positive things. But Alex doesn't wholly belong to this category. He can still remember some of the miserable experiences.

'It was an absolute miracle that the vehicles held together. We drove the American built Autocars, equipped with Caterpillar engines. They had a three-range gearbox, five gears in each. They weren't easy to drive. Cumbersome and heavy, but I don't think any other vehicle in the world would have stood up to the stresses and strains. They were large and yellow as I remember. We never found, by the way, any instruction manual so you had to use your instincts when something shook to pieces'.

Alex came to Africa 25 years ago. He has probably encountered just about everything a long-distance driver can dream about in his worst nightmares.

'Just take the roads. If we can use that expression, of course'. Alex laughed and finished his beer in one great gulp.

'During the rainy season we always drove in convoys. Otherwise we couldn't even have had a theoretical chance of getting up the hills'.

But don't jump to the conclusion that Alex and his colleagues towed one another up the hills. Their method was much more primitive than that!

'It was uphill and downhill. In the hollow between the two hills there was always a bridge. A miserable, fragile little bridge.

'The first truck drove down the hill as fast as he could. If he was lucky the bridge would hold. And if it was a good day, then he got more than half way up the slope before he came to a halt'. Alex twirled his moustache. He was a good storyteller, with a tendency to dramatic pauses.

'The second truck did the same thing. Full-speed downhill. With a little luck he would cross the bridge and drive straight into the back of the first truck, which hopefully shunted forward a little. And then it was the third truck's turn — the same manoeuvre. If we were lucky, the first truck would get a hold and be able to

pull the rest of us up. That's what I call teamwork'.

We listened to Alex and ought perhaps to have allowed for a little exaggeration. But we understood that the conditions must have been dreadful 25 years ago. As God only knows, it's not child's play getting over the African continent today. But 25 years ago . . . it's hardly possible to imagine what it must have been like.

'Sure the roads were pure hell'.

Alex had lowered his tone a bit. His face had taken on a more serious expression.

'It wasn't nature and the elements which jinxed us most. It was people. Now that I've got a better perspective on life and all the problems facing the new states, I understand perhaps a bit better. But at the time, I could have murdered every single policeman.

'At the time, the Liberian police were called sheriffs. Young African policemen with a mass of power built into their shoulderstraps.

'They could smell out foreign drivers.

Sometimes the bridges held, sometimes they didn't. As a trucker you always have to calculate the risks.

AN AFRICAN ADVENTURE

And they made our life a real misery. There was only one thing to do and that was stop if they raised their arms, something they did every other kilometer!

'The procedure was always the same. Driving licence! For six months I used my helicopter licence. Just to play the devil. But eventually I came across a sheriff who could read. And then I had to pay five times the usual bribe in order to continue driving. For bribes were what it was all about. If you didn't drop a coin in the hand of every sheriff who turned up in the jungle you didn't move a meter. Every day I forked out the equivalent of an annual income for a policeman.'

But the day came when Alex got tired of the whole thing. 'It was pointless to refuse to pay. You just ended up in a little cell with only spiders and snakes for company. And there you stayed until the company's helicopter tracked down the truck and got you released for some misdemeanour which you'd never actually committed.

'Then one day my patience ran out completely. It was a Saturday and I was on my way to Nimba, tired, filthy and hungry. I was nearly there when I was stopped by a sheriff. He'd parked his Fiat 500 straight across the road.

'There he stood, the big, tough sheriff, leaning against his car. He had a cigarette dangling from the corner of his mouth and his right hand was nonchalantly resting on his pistol holster.'

Alex had two alternatives: he could stop and pay, or he could drive his gigantic Autocar straight over the Fiat. Alex chose the latter.

'A Fiat 500 is like a young birch. All you have to do is lean against it. It looked completely different after I had finished with it I can assure you. A bit flat, if you get my meaning.'

Alex wound up his windows and gave it all he had to the terminal. Through a narrow window he persuaded an official to pay his pursuer.

'Then all that was left was to pack everything together and go home. Until I started to get itchy feet again to come back to Africa.'

The sun was low outside the windows of the Lune Rouge bar, but the traffic on the streets was still heavy. The tauregs, or the blue people of the Sahara as they are also called, were walking hand in hand on the pavements. They got their name from the indigo colour in their blackish-blue costumes. The colour eats into the skin because of the heat.

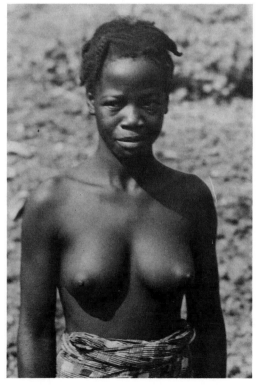

(Above) Apes can be trained to do a lot of things. Even to work as mechanics! But did they managed to change tyres?

(Left) It was still natural during the beginning of the 60's for African women to go around bare-breasted.

Over: Before the road network was more fully developed, the tracks were narrow and hard to follow. It was a matter of sharing what little space there was. Accidents were move than common. During development, planes flew workers and crew in and out of the more inaccessible areas.

AN AFRICAN ADVENTURE

We talked absent-mindedly about the trucker's life in Africa and shuddered at the thought of what might await us in Togo.

We had seen the Algerians' ability to survive out on the ring fence. They must be amongst the world's cleverest and most skilled. Far removed from the American and in many cases the European romantic view of trucking, the Algerians steer their heavy trailers between the holes in the roads. They roar along at high speed over the wash board surface.

Through some inexplicable miracle, they manage to keep their badly worn-out vehicles in one piece and almost always get them to work. They are masters at make-do repairs; and changing tyres is all part of the routine in the desert. During our shaky journey from Morocco through Algeria we saw hundreds of massacred tyres along the roadside.

The Australian gentleman with the red nose had grumbled about the lack of help in the desert. This applied to Europeans and other non-Africans. The Algerian long-distance trucks have an important service-function in the desert. They drive

(Opposite bottom and above)
The blistering sands of the Sahara offer a biting contrast to the tropical rain forests along the Equator.

(Opposite top) Many bridges had to be built. The bridges could stand up to the weight of the crew that built it, while heavy trucks always ran a risk.

(Left) There isn't much wood out in the desert. If you want a fire, you have to collect wood wherever you can find it.

Over: Men of the Sahara and their 'beasts of burden'.

AN AFRICAN ADVENTURE

hitch-hikers between the oases, fetch spare parts and help those who've got problems with their vehicles.

Whenever we stopped for a cuppa, an Algerian driver always stopped and asked if everything was OK.

We'd hardly left the comfortable wicker-work chairs before we heard the ringing sounds of our own mother tongue. Two sweaty, rather dirty youths came in through the door. They pronounced a few hoarse words, a barely recognizable request for beer. We introduced ourselves.

The two thirsty youths were no less than Göran Svensson and Björn Carlsson from Småland in southern Sweden.

The beautiful Tamanrasset night would have to wait. We sat down again in the creaking but comfortable wickerwork chairs.

'We've come from Nigeria and are on our way up to Tunisia, and if it hadn't been for two eggs we'd probably still be there.' We looked somewhat surprised at the two lads, who were greedily gulping down their beers.

'Well, we met a Dane who taught us the trick. You can fix a leaking radiator by cracking two eggs into the water. Soap is the best thing to use for a split tank'.

We made a note: eggs for a radiator, soap for a tank! Göran and Björn were travelling through Africa in an ex-fire-engine — a Unimog 62.

'It looks like a cross between a petrol depot and a tool shed. When we bought the Unimog it had already made a five-month journey through Africa. So it knows what it's all about.'

Göran and Björn got through without any serious scrapes. The fire-engine had survived the worst trials. Just like an echo from Alex, the two lads described the real problem: human greed.

'While in Kano, a town in northern Nigeria, we were accused of careless parking,' Björn tells us. 'But we couldn't see any difference between the way we'd parked and anybody else. But the police had their own special and decided point of view.

'The Chief of Police would have imprisoned us for life had he found out how nonchalantly and heedlessly we defied Kano's parking regulations. The only thing to do was to hop into the fire-engine and turn right for the gaol. Funnily enough, the way to prison always consists of right turns.

'Soon we were back at the scene of the crime. But the police soon found a smart solution'.

Göran took over the story.

'A gift to the chief of 50 naira (15 pounds sterling) would solve the problem. We thought the cell was a better alternative. After a few more turns to the right we were offered a unique special price of 20 naira — "The cell", was our answer. "We'll take the cell". Once we had gone as far as rejecting 5 naira the man was obviously about to go mad. It all ended with 50 kobo, enough for a taxi home. We realised that his pride wouldn't let him leave empty-handed.'

As dawn broke in the desert and the dogs awoke in Tamarasset, Ahmed banged on the door. The evening spent with Göran and Björn has been a late one. We'd almost forgotten Ahmed.

We'd met him a couple of days earlier, a genuine taureg. Ahmed was riding — or rather 'jogging' — on his dromedary in a dried-up river furrow. You could hardly see his face for his dark blue turban.

Ahmed took us to his neat little reed and tree-branch plaited house, and we suddenly remembered why he banged on our door. In a moment of weakness we had promised to help him move some bricks to his new house. With our large Mercedes we could do it in one load. It took us a day and this was yet one more reason for postponing the journey to Togo. And in a moment of weakness we also promised Ahmed's brother the same favour. Togo seems even further away now.

But everything comes to an end, as did our relaxed stay in the pearl of Algeria, Tamanrasset. We counted our money and decided that we'd definitely been fleeced far too heavily. Our only consolation was that it's an everyday occurence for a European in Africa.

Alex had had to pay.

Alright, Göran and Björn had been able to argue, but they'd had to pay up all the same.

In front of us are Mali and Niger. Two states and then little Togo.

(Left top) Road-work in Africa demands heavy machinery. Often rugged terrain has to be overcome before the road can be completed.

(Left bottom) When Liberia's roads were constructed, many of the road-workers were not accustomed to trucks. Accidents were a part of the wildest, most rugged terrain.

Over: The Sahara roads are marked out by sticks stuck into the ground along the roadbed.

AN AFRICAN ADVENTURE

chapter 8

HELL'S RALLY PARIS-DAKAR

(Right) The rally runs through different terrain, from the heart of Paris to Dakar in Senegal. But the real terror is the Sahara. Most are forced to 'bite the dust' along this particular stretch.

Over: The Paris-Dakar used to be 'hell-race' with one's life as the stake. Today, the rally through the blistering desert carries less risks even though it is still very, very rugged.

**HELL'S RALLY
PARIS-DAKAR**

I f you stand on the Place de la Concorde in the heart of Paris you won't have any trouble seeing the Greek temple facade of the Church of Madelein, nor the obelisk raised by Napoleon I after he carried it off from Egypt.

The exploits of Napoleon felt a little symbolic that early January morning.

The French have always had an eye for opportunity — they have never made any secret of the role they played, and expect to play, in world affairs.

The Place de la Concorde — maybe the most impressive square in the world — is a good example of this.

The reason for the day's gathering in the square was the reconquest of West Africa. The Colonies are of course long gone, and the governor of West Africa isn't seated in his opulent throne down in Dakar, either. But the road to it is still open.

You could always fly down there, and gaze down on the Algerian and Moroccan deserts from 10,000 feet up.

Or you can take the car.

But, you don't have to drive all the way through Algeria, Niger, Upper Volta, the Ivory Coast, Guinea, Mali, or Mauretania just to reach Dakar in Senegal, unless you want to get a clear picture of the impressive expanse of territory that France held before 1960.

You can just as easily take the road through Tchad, The Central African Republic, Congo, and Gabon, but then you'd have to cross through the ex-British colony of Nigeria. That wouldn't be quite right. Certainly not very French.

You see, the toughest automobile race in the world is French. That's something we never doubted as we made our way through the masses of filmstars, musicians, singers and other celebrities at the Place de la Concorde that morning.

Even the first French astronaut was revving up at the startline, right beside President Mitterand's private chauffeur.

The craziest race the world has ever seen was just about to start!

Hell's Rally, from Paris to Dakar . . . .

Those who have made the trip before know what's in store. They can probably feel the sand gritty and hot between their teeth, feel their eyes practically bursting out of their sockets, their kidneys begging for mercy.

There were some people out on the starting line who were be making their sixth trip. They were along for the chase back in 1979 during the Premier rally.

You didn't have to pass through Guinea then.

If it really matters, that is.

253 cars, 31 trucks, and 114 motorcycles stood ready on the line. Only a fraction of them will ever see Dakar.

The Paris-Dakar Rally is about 10,000 kilometers long, and is split up into special sections. It's well-known that before Agades, in Niger, half of the contestants quit the race — the Sahara puts fear in a man.

'I wouldn't do the Sahara race again for a million dollars!', the Danish writer and Africa expert, Joergen Bitsch once said.

When he was ready to take off through Africa in a car for the 27th time, no less, one of his friends was stupefied.

'I wouldn't do it for a million dollars' Joergen explained, 'I do it for the sheer excitement of it all!'

Many adventurers have paid for the excitement with their lives. Some have died while desperately gulping radiator fluid, rusty and bitter. Others poured poisonous brake fluid down their throats before the sun dried out their bodies.

Well, nobody was going to run into that kind of trouble this time around. The Paris—Dakar Rally is a people's festival, nobody is allowed to just disappear into the shifting sands. Every kilometer is watched from the air. No, nowadays, it's a battle for survival — of machines.

(Above) The rally runs through the shifting desert, with only an occasional oasis to break the monotony. A really grueling trip, even for the most experienced.

(Right) The desert is beautiful as well as treacherous. Anybody who takes on the Paris-Dakar has to know what he's getting into; but the adventure is too exciting to be put off.

HELL'S RALLY PARIS-DAKAR

A very special talent is required for Sahara driving. Not to mention a large degree of self-control. There are long stretches of loose shifting sands, causing a vehicle to dig itself down if one drives too slowly. On the other hand, if you drive too fast, you lose control and the risk of overturning is increased.

The dangers are innumerable. After shaking one's insides to jelly driving over rocky terrain, the flat endless expanse before you looks like a mirage. Most likely, one won't see the gaping crack in the sand until too late. Cars are generally pounded into junk around here.

That's exactly what happened to the 1984 public's favourite in the heavy class. Dutchman Jan de Rooy, who with his unusual DAF FA 3300 was attempting to repeat his victory of 1982, had to throw in the towel, after one of his axles broke off on the stretch between Tamanrasset in Algeria and Iferoune in Niger. Despite carrying two engines, two driveshafts, and 800 horsepower, the desert won hands down.

Nothing turns out as one expects. Irregardless of the full support of a financially solid pit-crew, nature takes her toll.

For some, it all goes to hell even before the fun begins.

Jean-Loup Chretien, the French astronaut who floated around up there with the Russians, found it wise to quit before he reached the desert. His back-up vehicle missed no less than three checkpoints in France, and the spectre of being left alone out there in the sands made him reconsider.

Sand, rocks, and a blood-red boiling sun. One by one they dropped from the list. Some called it quits when they realized they couldn't read the 300 page thick route manual.

Naturally it's written in French!

Some just get tired of the bureaucracy. The Algerian authorities materialized new rules calling for mandatory currency exchange as well as a new fuel-coupon system that had all contestants paying double.

At the Upper Volta border some heavy rigs stood idling for hours until the Customs officials decided to give them the go ahead.

In Guinea, a sudden rule change barred all trucks from the charted route of the Rally . . ..

Even the people have to be defeated.

The entry into Dakar is a procession of real triumph, for those who against all odds have made it that far. The fortified city on the South side of Cape Verde was in bedlam from the Carnival atmosphere. People jumped on the cars, yelling and shouting, as the caravan of 'survivors' into the city.

First to cross the line was a Porsche, driven by the legendary Jacky Ickz.

First of the heavies was a Mercedes.

With it's mighty ten-cylinder engine at 18.27 liters and 355 horsepower, Mercedes 1936 AK 4x4 repeated its triumph of 1983. Behind the wheel sat another legendary desert-fox, Laleu. The motorcycle class was won by BMW.

The night was a long one. The celebration of those who actually made it all the way was incredible to see, and seemingly never-ending!

Along the 10,000 kilometers back to Paris, the wrecks and shambles of the 'also-rans' clearly showed the death-struggle between nature and machine.

A battle that nature may also lose.

The question is, who won this round?

It's clear, that irregardless of back-up vehicles, helicopters, and bank-rolled pit-crews, it was a close finsh.

The short line of smashed and battered machines that trundled across the finish line was not an impressive sight.

It didn't help at all when Lada's French importer, Poch, invested millions in order to see his great hope, Bernard Darniche, win — Darniche didn't even make it to the Algerian oasis of Tamarnasset.

Or take the case of Jean-Pierre Jabouille, the Formula One driver who was to win, just in case Darniche didn't pull through — he collapsed before he reached Inazaoua.

And it sure didn't help when IVECO hired French firefighters in order to coax their rigs through the burning sands — one smashed his front-axle. The other two were disqualified.

It looked as though nature had won this round?

This year . . . .

Over: When the desert dust has worked its way up nostrils, around eyes, and grits between one's teeth, then you know the rally is starting to show its true colours. It's now that a driver has to prove that man is stronger than the elements!

HELL'S RALLY PARIS-DAKAR

chapter 9

AN ARABIAN ENCOUNTER

It was Sunday in Tartus, Syria, when the truck ferry steered into the harbour. Over at another berth a Russian submarine and its flagship lay rolling gently, while a short distance away the latest shipment of Russian arms was being unloaded. A cold, sandy wind blew as the ferry nudged itself into position and lowered the ramp.

Among those who rolled off was Christer Dahllöf, from Voeroebacka, Sweden; a veteran of the Saudi trade. He drives for Vebe-Trans of Varberg, Sweden. He made his first trip to Saudi Arabia back in 1979 — nowadays he does 'the trip' ten times a year.

'Now don't go writing a bunch of romantic balderdash!' Christer exclaimed to me.

'Driving the Saudi route is just a job. Maybe a little more difficult or trickier than others, but still just a job.

'The ones who tell you all the wild tales are the ones that have driven one trip and lived on it for the rest of their lives,' he went on.

We'd left Sweden by way of Trelleborg, cruised through East Germany and Czechoslovakia to the music of Charlie Pride and Conway Twitty, with ten tonnes on the trailer. The F 12, which Christer bought in 1980, rumbled along down through Austria to the port of Koper in Yugoslavia.

It took four days from Koper to cross the Mediterranean by truck ferry. We'd enjoyed the sunshine at 18 knots down past Crete and Cyprus. We arrived in Asia — and this was when the rules changed.

'It has gotten a lot more difficult since my first trip,' Christer told me. 'The Customs in Tartus is a good example. It was alright until a Swede was caught smuggling weapons. Then all hell broke loose; for a while every Scandinavian trucker had to open up the whole load for inspection!'

'In Saudi Arabia, it is the Austrian 'booze-rigs' that have caused all the trouble. They smuggle booze in the space between the walls of the refrigerator-trailers. But the Customs people generally find what they're looking for. In Hadita, the border station between Saudi Arabia and Jordan, they sometimes shoot holes through the roof of a suspect vehicle. Sometimes the booze drips out, sometimes not.

'The toughest method they use is to just drive a fork-lift through the trailer wall. If there's anything in there, they'll find it for sure . . .' he went on.

(I have to admit, I thought old Christer was 'laying it on a bit thick', but I got the opportunity to see it happen with my own eyes ten days later . . .).

I stepped off the ferry in order to get a good shot of Christer as he drove down the ramp. For safety's sake I asked Jerry, the ship's agent in Tartus, if it was OK to take pictures.

'You must be out of your mind!' he mumbled tiredly from behind his sunglasses . . ..

'The last time any pictures were taken around here was when a rig got damaged coming off the ramp. I told the trucker to take some shots for the claims people. Then I spent the next three days trying to get him out of the local jail!'

I stuffed my camera out of sight in a real hurry, and jumped into the cab beside Christer. In Syria you play by Syrian rules — not any others.

When we'd finally inched our way clear of the harbour, we drove up to 'Grandpa' — an old Arab with a combined restaurant/barber/currency exchange and fence operation. His place is a rendez-vous for Scandinavian trukers down in the Middle East. A stones throw away lie the offices of the Ferry line. They translate all documents into Ara-

bic, check passports and stamp them, and collect fees and dues. When the ferry is at dock the line into that office looks about ten miles long!

Patience is the name of the game for a trucker on the Middle East trade. Countless papers and documents have to be shown and reshown, and pass inspection at innumerable border stations, where Customs officials don't seem to sling their pistols for the fun of it . . . .

'Bokhra in'nsh'Allah', is the usual answer to all questions — 'Tomorrow if Allah wills it'.

But we ran into some luck. After having found Christer's passport, which a German trucker had been given by mistake, we were free to roll, after a sleepless night.

The road from Tartus to Homs was a nightmare, narrow and winding, but happily it was still dark and there wasn't much traffic. The only real problem was parked cars; they don't use their parking lights, they place big rocks out in the road about a hundred meters from where they're parked. You notice these rocks, believe me.

After 20 miles or so we ran into something that just blew my mind — a rig with red lights on the cab roof, along the

Construction material being unloaded. Everything must be intact, even the most sensitive instruments.

Over:

(Left top) The morning convoy to Saudi Arabia leaves at eight o'clock from Ramta in Jordan, 200 kilometers before the border.

(Left bottom) A common sight along the roads throughout Saudi Arabia, a Mosque. One entrance for women. One for men. All shoes are left outside.

(Right top) Christer Dahllöf on his way home. He carried a load of springs picked up from an old steel mill in Judenburg, Austria.

(Right bottom) A typical 'jalla-rig'. A grey-green Mercedes with high, colorful wooden slats and lots of lamps.

AN ARABIAN ENCOUNTER

(Above) Road-works in Saudi Arabia. A guy with a red flag warned us: 'Slow Down'!

(Right top) Yet another 'jallarig' down the long straight desert highways.

(Right bottom) 'Saudi Arabia, Love it or Leave it', reads the decal on this Finnish trucker's shirt. Life as a trucker in the Middle East couldn't be better described.

Over: Coffee-break in the sun is at high noon and it is HOT. A trucker in the Middle East lives just as hard a life as his counterparts in the Australian desert.

AN ARABIAN ENCOUNTER

cab sides and along the grille, and blue headlights!

'You just wait until we get into Saudi Arabia. There you can't tell the front from the back of them!' Christer laughed.

We rolled through Damascus right in the middle of the 11 o'clock rush hour. On the way south towards Dera and the Jordanian border we drove past at least a hundred Russian tanks all trundling along in the same direction.

There are several checkpoints along the road. The Middle East isn't exactly the quietest place in the world nowadays.

A speciality of the Arab world is the 'sleeping policemen' — a ten inch ridge across the road. The only way to cross one of them is by stopping then crawling over it with all wheels on lowest gear and pray that you'll see the next one in time as well.

We were met by a flock of boys at the Dera border station. Christer is well-known to the children around here. They do 'favours' — run with papers and documents, fix passports, 'guard the truck', for a flat fee of five Syrian pounds. Not everybody pays, but Christer gets a kick out of helping the kids out, so he's remembered and liked.

For once there wasn't a two-mile queue, so we were quickly across the

border into Jordan, and rolled into the border town of Ramta.

Next morning the rigs lined up for the early convoy. Anyone going to Saudi Arabia travels in a convoy under the watchful eyes of the military over the 270 miles to the next border. There were Lebanese hauling 40 tonnes of cedar-wood, Austrians driving for LKW Walter, English, Germans, Danes, and of course, ourselves — all in the trade with goods and merchandise for the Saudis or the Arab Emirates farther down the coast along the Gulf.

The rigs roll in heavily loaded, and rumble home empty. Day in and day out, week by week. The freight flows in a never-ending stream, all paid for by the precious oil.

This convoy is probably the toughest 'rally' in the world. 150 rigs, all with one goal — first to the border — nobody gives anything away on this route.

On the 'home stretch', just before one reaches the Saudi town of Hadita, it's like an insane cavalry charge — eight or nine rigs abreast charging out of the boiling sand, and all hanging on the horn.

Hadita is a border station beyond comparison — every single piece of freight is taken off the truck and

inspections are carried out on empty rigs. It can take a week, sometimes more, to get through the eye of this needle. Some people never get to leave.

'They still pinch the occasional smuggler down here; the last fool hasn't been born yet . . .' Christer mutters.

It was raining, windy and cold. March weather that might be passable somewhere else, but down here it just didn't fit into the desert vision I've built up inside myself! I shivered under my thin pullover and pulled my scarf tighter around my chin.

All around the convoy, piles of freight were collecting on the ground. Tired truckers helped out with the unloading, some Egyptian forwarders were running around with documents. Saudi Bedouins, functioning as Customs officials wandered around gazing with scorn upon the 'unclean' as the European Christian truckers are called.

Once again we ran into some luck. After two days and nights, we managed to get an official to look through the load and stamp our documents. Christer's ten tonnes were made up of building materials for BPA, four huge electrical generators from ASEA for a South Korean hospital in Riyadh, and some crates for SAUDI

ASPHALT in Jeddah.

We stowed the cargo in record time and rolled ·out into the Saudi desert, still smarting from resounding kisses on each cheek from Vebe-Trans Arabian forwarding agent, Al Rajeh.

The sound of the air-conditioner blended with the throaty rumble from Christer's 350 horsepower under the hood. We were pointed towards Turaif 'pipeline road', and Arar. The desert is flat and uneventful; it really does remind one of an ocean — just like the Mediterranean, junk and the flotsam and jetsam of earlier trips litter the sands; old tyres, wrecks, oil-spills and plastic bags. Occasionally we glimpsed the silhouette of a Bedouin tent on the horizon, like some Chinese junk ventured too far west.

Many Middle Eastern truckers have had stints as sailors before catching the 'truckers blues'. I can clearly see why.

'The loneliness is the worst thing, in the beginning. You ached for another human being, after sitting behind the wheel for a week with nobody to talk to. Nowadays, I'd just as soon gas along all by myself. There's just something about a cup of tea all alone out in the middle of the desert . . .' Christer said pensively.

We were running south-east, headed for Al Batin, from there we veered southwards towards the capital of Riyadh. It was getting hotter, and we met a constant stream of Mercedes rigs. However, five times during the day all traffic stops. The rigs pull out into the desert and the drivers unroll their prayer mats. For the muslims, this is compulsory.

It was still 'winter' in the desert. The Bedouin women were gathering slivery stalks of grass in order to feed the goats and camels when the sun has burnt out all the vegetation later in the season.

Here and there we saw piles of steel rings lying about in the sand. Christer explained:

'When the Arabian truckers think it's getting too chilly, they just set fire to an old tyre'.

The night draws the animals out on to the roads. The Asphalt retains the heat from the day longer than the desert sand and gravel. Mice, snakes, and lizards come creeping out on to the roadbed — unfortunately, so do the camels. Christer doesn't drive at night.

We caught on to the 'desert rhythm' pretty fast — up with the sun around six in the morning, hammer down until about 12 noon, a half hour break, then hammer down some more until the sun

sets about six o' clock in the evening 12 or 13 hours a day is normal down here.

There are other truckers in this trade who drive longer. Christer sleeps at night. Other Saudi drivers drive more or less around the clock, which is less than sensible.

At regular intervals we came across small 'stations' with a tent pitched in the middle. Around the tent stood parts of the Saudi 'sand crew'. Road graders, dumpers and assorted rigs. Occasionally the Saudis have to remove the sand dunes that blow across the roads.

1700 miles from Hadita, we arrived at Riyadh, unload at BPA, and Christer telephoned back to his base. The generators are unloaded as well, and now the rig was almost empty.

'It's not so bad unloading her now,' Christer smiled, 'but come down here and help tear off her tarps in 115 degrees F later on in the season. It's not something to make a man laugh, that's for sure!'

Early next morning we were on our way towards Jeddah and the Red Sea. The villages along the road are small. Usually little houses clustered around a police station and a small café. We tore up a boiling cloud of choking dust as we blasted along. The roads here are wide and straight.

We pulled up about dusk at a filling station to buy something cold to drink. The heat slammed against us when we climbed down from the cab. We were immediately invited to have some 'shay' (tea). Hospitality is a virtue, and is a rule that pertains to the 'unclean' as well out here in the desert. Trouble doesn't make distinctions based on religion. In the desert all are brothers and are honour-bound to help and serve each other. That's a Saudi Arabian law, as a matter of fact.

Marat, Shokra, Afif, Salim, Taif. The villages rose up out of the sands and were swallowed in the dust behind us. Soon we were in Jeddah, the city with the giant harbour, and the world's largest airport (three times larger than JFK in New York City).

After surmounting the usual problems of finding anything — street signs are as unusual as city roadmaps in Saudi Arabia — we managed to get our crates unloaded, and turned the Volvo around, ready for the Jordanian border run. Christer checked by telex to see when the ship from Tartus, Syria to Europe would be leaving. The answer made us a little worried — it would leave on Friday. It was Tuesday. Ahead of us lied 2700 miles through Saudi Arabia, 280 miles through Jordan, and

(Right top) A trucker in Asia soon learns that it is often a matter of waiting. The redtape is long and no one seems to be in any hurry.

(Right bottom) Sometimes you run across animals along and on the roads. This donkey refused to move. Maybe she was waiting for a cooling breeze from the passing rig?

AN ARABIAN ENCOUNTER

about 420 miles through Syria. Was it possible to reach Tartus in two and a half days? It had to be!

'You picked a fine time to leave me, Lucille . . .' Kenny Rogers blasted form the 40 watt speakers, as we travelled along a dried up river bed on our way to Medina. The trailer was empty and we were on our way home! The rig seemed to hum in appreciation! There was a lot of traffic. Jeddah handles a lot of freight, unloaded from ships for trucking up to Tabuk or Riyadh. We met several Macks, Kenworths and Volvos — even though Mercedes is by far the most common rig out here.

After an area of sand dunes, some high as mountains, the desert again flattened leaving nothing for the eyes to focus upon. An occasional date palm oasis shimmered in the distance.

One night we listened to the outrageous roar of an angry donkey close by us, as we sat in the parked rig before dropping off to sleep. Next morning we discovered that we'd stopped in the middle of an amazed Bedouin camp!

But now it was kidney-stomping hard driving — the Jordanian border was soon behind us. We made Syria in a hop, skip and jump. And into dear old Tartus again.

For about the fiftieth time on this trip we were lucky . . .. We got the last tickets to the ship, which was to arrive Friday night. We had just made a record-breaking run up from Jeddah, and in four days we'd be in Europe again.

Over: Fill her up. Diesel costs almost nothing in Saudi Arabia! Fuel price includes transport from the refinery to the gas stations and costs for the station. The fuel itself is free.

AN ARABIAN ENCOUNTER

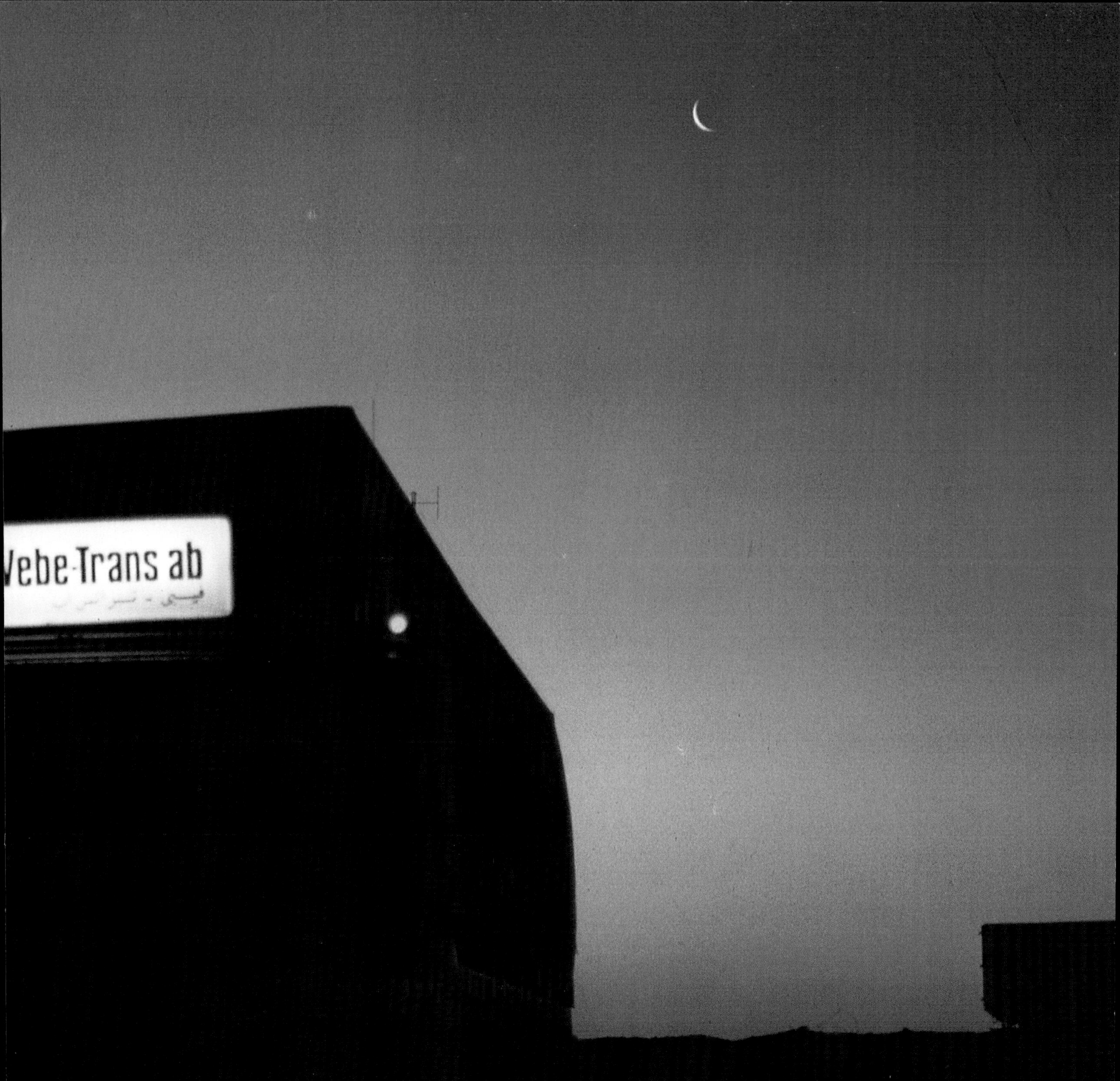
Vebe-Trans ab

chapter 10

TRUCKSTOP AMERICA

Where bustling, chaotic Tijuana meets the border to the USA, and Mexican poverty gives way to the dazzling, extravagant prosperity of California; that's where the freeway starts.

The Interstate 5 stretches all the way to the small town of Blaine on the Canadian border. The beautiful coastal stretch along the Pacific shores, through Long Beach and Los Angeles is just the beginning.

San Francisco with its majestic bridges flickers by in the west. The states of Oregon and Washington consume both tyres and time.

It's a route full of beauty and history. A route that has seen the mad days of the gold rush and the relentless laws of the wild west.

This was the goal of the fortune hunters and adventurers. This was the land of the settlers.

Today there are no horses left — just horsepower. But the adventurers are still here. Sometimes they wear the hat and boots. Their gun is usually close at hand. History has just changed its guise a little.

A hundred years ago Buttonwillow very probably had its own casino and saloon. Fair ladies offered their services to the wandering cattle-drivers and aimless adventurers. Bourbon whisky flowed, clearing the dust from dry mouths and throats. The odd poker gang sat and played. Perhaps one of Butch Cassidy's Wild Bunch stood leaning over the bar with a hunted look in his eye, worried that Allan Pinkerton, the master detective, was on a witch-hunt.

There are no lathered horses tied up today at Buttonwillow water-hole. Instead, the entrance is packed with powerful, shining Kenworths, Peterbilts, Freightliners, Whites, Ford GMCs, Internationals and the odd Mack.

Our truckstop was north of Los Angeles, just north-west of Bakerfield, where the Interstate 5 sets its almost dead straight course towards San Francisco. In Buttonwillow, where history has left its mark for good.

We stepped outside the door and scouted in vain for buckets and saloon doors. Instead, we only saw fuel depots, car washes, workshops and motel after

For those who are good with a brush, who can lacquer a fine text or motif, a rig can be paradise. There's always something that has to be done, some idea that makes the paint-job even better.

Over: A truckstop has to attract customers. To a tired trucker, a truckstop is like the proverbial 'light at the end of a long, dark tunnel'. Here at last he can get a much needed cup of coffee, a hamburger, and a chance to talk with other truckers.

TRUCKSTOP AMERICA

(Above) Every trucker has his goal, every load has it's destination. And at the truckstop people meet, whether the trip is to Mexico or Washington State.

Over:

(Left top) At the truckstop, you can give your rig a quick overhaul and repairs.

(Middle) If you can't take an ordinary vacation, there's always the alternative of packing the family into the cab.

TRUCKSTOP AMERICA

motel. The petrol pumps shouted out their special offers and the discounts outside the spare-parts shops tried to out do one another.

Bill from Oregon pushed his hat over his forehead, dabbed his neck with a cloth, and said as if he had read our thoughts, 'Here on the west coast it's important to keep your rig looking smart.'

We cast our eyes over the well-polished chrome on the Peterbilt and nodded in appreciation.

'It seems to be that the police here in this state only stop scruffy, dirty vehicles', Bill continued with an explanatory smile. 'It's important to look as good as possible.'

A few blokes came to help Bill and

were polishing for all they're worth.

Mark from Buttonwillow — where everything revolves around trucks and the truckstop — cleaned and polished as if his like depended on it. His only source of income is vehicle maintenance.

'It's not so bad', said Mark stopping for a short break. 'If I'm lucky I can make up to 40 or 50 dollars a day. It's mostly minor repairs, bulb-changes and chrome-polishing. There's no fixed rate, the driver just pays as much as he feels like.'

We realised that Mark's last comment wasn't aimed at us. A small hint to Bill from Oregon, who'd soon have to foot the bill.

We went in to get a cuppa and landed

right in the middle of the lunch rush. The waitresses, with steaming hot pots of coffee, were running each other off their feet. Top-ups are free. Like everywhere else in California.

A tempting smell floated out from the charcoal grills in the kitchen. And right in the middle of the smokey confusion you could glimpse cheese burgers, bacon burgers, Bergundy burgers, supreme burgers, zesty burgers, nifty burgers, braun burgers, blue ribbon burgers, caraway burgers and crunchy teriyaki burgers.

We hope you'll forgive us if we've forgotten any combination. The main ingredients are the same anyway: top quality mince, onions, mustard, horse-radish and Worcestershire sauce.

We sat down next to Mick Jones from Indiana, ordered one of the exotic burgers and were told 'sure love' when we quietly asked if we could have chilli con carne with our burgers.

'The best grub in the whole state', Mick said as he swigged his Budweiser slowly but with enjoyment.

He rubbed the froth away with the back of his hand and gave us a broad smile.

The barriers were down. We didn't even have to give him a cue. 'I carry different poisons and can't drive on weekends. So I usually make sure I get as far as Buttonwillow.'

(Right top)Any truckstop that wants to survive the competition has to provide excellent service. One or two mechanics on call is the least to be expected.

(Left bottom) At least in western USA, the police seem to have nothing but good marks for clean rigs.

(Right bottom) Where tired cowpokes once watered their herds, now stand Kenworths, Internationals, Macks, Peterbilts, and other models.

TRUCKSTOP AMERICA

Mick shouted to the waitress who, despite the general hum and noise, understood that he wanted another Budweiser.

'Fantastic service. But I bet they earn a bit. There aren't many who drive past Buttonwillow.'

And it certainly looked like it. It was Friday but the place was full to bursting point all the same.

'There are lots that think like me', Mick said as he pushed the empty plate away which had once had the half a pound burger on it.

'If you have to put up somewhere for the weekend this is one of the best choices.'

Our burgers tasted great, of course. Think what you can do with a hamburger. The thin, light, ice-cold beer ran easily down the throat. Mick did all the talking.

'Your first time in Buttonwillow?'

We didn't need to answer. Mick Jones was taking care of us. Once again we enjoyed American hospitality, the almost naive but truly sincere desire to make foreigners feel at home.

Mick suggested the bar and perhaps a game of pool.

'It's on me.'

He thumped us on the back. We pushed our way through the sea of people. It was not long before were at the Buttonwillow waterhole. The bar.

It was dark in the bar. The neon signs with beer adverts gave a magic atmosphere to the five meters long bar counter. Wendy, enthroned amongst the bottles and beer barrels, mixed drinks and sent frothy tankards over the counter.

The jukebox only seemed to play country and western: Willie Nelson, Waylon Jennings, Loretta Lynn and Johnny Cash. You can hear the clatter of the billiard balls in the background.

Mick mumbled his order and the ice cubes were soon jangling in the glass. We looked at each other and gulped down the contents.

There were a number of local farming lads in the 150 kg class crowded in amongst the drivers. People were just passing the time of day, enjoying the somewhat humid, malt-smelling environment which characterizes American bars.

Someone raised his voice and we smelt trouble. But Mick put his hands firmly on our shoulders.

'Don't be worried lads,' he said

(Opposite top) Once in awhile, a truck from Mexico finds its way to the truckstop.

(Opposite bottom) In the old days, they wore wide-brimmed hats and had Colt Peacemakers hanging from their hips; today only the Colts have disappeared.

(Left top) A trucker might just need a little soul-searching claim some. The truth of it is that a lot of truckers seem to appreciate the holy word at the truckstop.

(Left bottom) The 'Truck Wash' sign appears like a mirage in the desert. Here one can finally give the rig a much needed wash and get her ready to roll down the next stretch of road.

Over: A good looking rig means a lot to the driver, who handles it with special care.

TRUCKSTOP AMERICA

calmingly. 'There's an unwritten law here. Have as much fun as you like, but never at someone else's expense. If you start trouble then you're out head first, with a kick in the backside as extra help.'

We sneaked a look at Wendy and wondered how she would manage a fight should it blow up.

'Her husband's in there.' Mick pointed at the door behind the bar counter. 'And a shot-gun under the counter.'

We leant over to see if Mick was telling the truth. All we saw was bottles and glasses.

'It's not often anything happens', Mick affirmed. Everybody knows that everybody else is armed'. In days gone by colts hung in a holster. Nowadays, refined firearms are hidden in jacket pockets and boot legs. History, as we said earlier, has taken on a different guise. It's just the people who haven't changed.

It was our round next, even if Mick did protest. We ordered a few beers. Here you just order beer and bourbon whisky. Everything else is women's drink.

There were virtually no parking spaces left. Lunch was slowly developing into afternoon and early evening. The drivers

hung around their vehicles, talking about the day and taking the opportunity to fill their log books.

Some were checking brakes and tyres before going into the showers with a towel over their shoulders. One driver was going round dishing out bills advertising a prayer meeting the following day. He was well received.

'I was saved four years ago', said John Perry while sticking a bill in our hands. 'We meet every Saturday, those of us who want to top up our spiritual batteries.'

John told us that his meetings are always well-attended.

'Jam-packed', whispered Mick, who by this time had moved out from the bar to the car park.

There seems to be a surprisingly large interest in religion among American truckers. 'Ours is a lonely job', John explained. 'Most of the lads appreciate a bit of spiritual guidance.'

A female driver pulled in with a puncture in one tyre. In two minutes flat the service truck had got to work with a tyre-change. Mick saw our surpirse at the speed of the operation.

'Don't run away with the idea that it's

(Opposite and this page):

The truckers come from every corner of the USA. From anywhere there's a load to be picked up, to anywhere where a load can be discharged. For a lonesome trucker, the truckstop isn't just a place to check over the rig and grab a bite to eat. It is also a place where he can trade experiences and stories with other truckers along the route.

Over: The truck is my home, or so the truckers say. And one's home should be clean and neat, with all the comforts and decorations. But these 'homes' must be kept in tip-top working condition.

TRUCKSTOP AMERICA

151

TRUCKSTOP AMERICA

just because she's a woman', said Mick. 'Here service is everything. The day the lads fail to get decent service they'll go elsewhere. And that would mean the end of Buttonwillow.'

We sauntered over to the punctured vehicle and said hello to Mary, who was busy putting on her boots. The stereo was roaring in the driver's seat — the old Elvis tunes almost seem to have been written for truckers.

Mary gave her credit card to the service crew.

'On my way to San Francisco. Just stopped because of the tyre. I'll be on the road again after a cup of coffee. I've got a full load of furniture that's got to be in Frisco before dawn.'

We sauntered slowly between the vehicles and found ourselves in the lubrication workshop. On a sign we saw that people here work round the clock, all the year round.

Two mechanics were on duty that night and both were busy fixing a short circuit on one vehicle and greasing another.

The lads were around 25 and clowning around so much that the waiting vehicle owners could hardly stop themselves laughing.

The two drivers waiting were both veterans from the state of Washington. The Interstate 5 lay ahead of them, their only way home.

'I started driving in 1946', said Yabo Johnson. 'In those days you could keep your foot down through all the states. Full speed ahead. No messing around. But today 90 km is the maximum speed and in every state you have to have a permit carefully tucked away in your wallet just to be able to do your job. And we've never earned as little as we do today. It's incredible really that we've got the strength to go on.'

Yabo admitted that he was feeling particularly negative, but he does, of course, have one or two things that he's justified in complaining about.

'Sure he's right'.

Willie Jackson, who had been listening to Yabo's complaints, was in agreement: 'Diesel's gone up by 200 per cent in the space of just a few years. But transport costs are just the same'.

Willie's GMC has gone 400,000 km without any major problems.

'Thank God', he sighed. 'There's quite simply no room in the budget for extensive repairs. And a new truck is out of the question. I haven't paid off the loan on this hulk yet.'

'No, America's not what she was', said Yabo, lighting a long green cigar. 'You can't even smoke the cigars these days'. Yabo spat out the bitten-off end of his cigar, gave a wry smile, but broke out suddenly into a wide, rumbling laugh.

'But why complain. As long as you've got food on the table and the old bowels keep moving, yes, then you can even sleep well at night.'

And Yabo seems to sleep well. We asked to take a peak at his sleeper.

'Sure!'

Yabo opened the door and started showing us the sleeper. There's not much lacking. If anything. The walls are covered in soft textile wallpapers. There's a radio, cassette-recorder, TV and video, toilet, sink, shower with hot and cold running water, fridge, microwave oven and a wide bed for Yabo's wide body.

'Who the hell has said that you can't have a comfortable life even if you are on the road? Why should I need to put in at a motel when I can sleep in my own bed, between my own sheets? My truck is my home.'

Yabo and Willie decided to stay the night in Buttonwillow. Willie at one of the ten motels. Yabo of course in his truck.

'But first a bite to eat', Yabo chuckled. 'It's on me.'

We were still feeling the effects of the hamburgers but understand that you can't say no to an offer from Yabo.

Yabo and Willie couldn't decide where to go. There are ten or so places to choose from. Eventually, we ended up in a booth, among the town's large, fresh salads and tasty, rare steaks.

We listened to Yabo and Willie. Yabo had long since snapped out of his depressed mood, and the longer the evening went on the funnier and less likely his stories became.

And while the mist rolled in over Buttonwillow, and silence fell over the water-hole, the neon signs went out one after the other. One or two brave souls tottered out from bars and restaurants on their way to an impersonal motel bed or their own cosy cabin.

In a few hours silence took over Buttonwillow. We dreamt about cattle-drivers.

Whether they were in the form of colt-armed long-distance riders with the four-legged form of horsepower, or truckers with several hundred hp under the bonnet.

You never know which way the wind's going to blow.

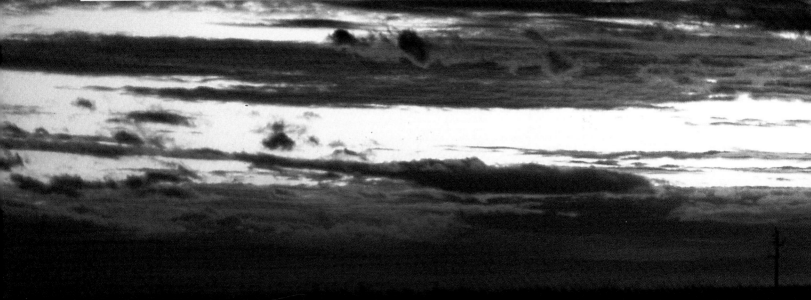

chapter 11

TRUCKERS ONBOARD

He leaned his heavy body against the reception desk. His old, washed-out jeans hung limply after yet another battle with the bulge. His T-shirt should have been an extra extra large, but too many bouts with the washer had given it its unusual shape.

A day-old stubble covered his chin, his eyes were heavy and vacant.

He was about to fall asleep any second. The desk clerk saved him just in time.

With a tired nod he took his key and his feet shuffled dejectedly across the lobby carpet. Our last glimpse was of him slowly receding into the endless hallways of the jumbo ferry.

He probably fell asleep in just a few minutes, and nothing in the world could have woken him. He'd have stayed like that until the automatic wake up call bawled its morning honky tonk music about eight hours later.

Just a worn-out guy who just managed to hammer down the autobahn in time to make the eleven o'clock ferry.

The next day he was behind the wheel once again.

The big wheels aren't always enough — nature hasn't been all that kind to the transport industry.

However, it isn't likely that this man somewhere deep in the ship's innards had any thoughts of that at all during his passage over the Baltic Straits!

But he just might have mumbled a quiet phrase of gratitude to the stately vessel that so safely carried him on his mission.

Life as a trucker would be noticeably different without ships.

We were gazing down on the quay at Travemünde from our positions at the rail. In just half an hour the huge ferry would slip its moorings and, guided by computers, would slowly slide out of the harbour. To the East, we'd be able to see the searchlights of the East German borderguards scheming tirelessly in their search for escapees from the totalitarian state's freedom! To the West we'd see the glimmer and shimmer of the casinos along the shore, with the Jaguars and Porsches lined up outside.

They were still loading below us. All autos had already been driven aboard, and were in orderly rows hanging from elevator platforms overhead; then the last few trucks slowly climb up the ramp and into the ferry. The ramp made an intolerable racket as its beams jumped and slammed.

(Right) The ferry is a link between continents. A necessity when wheels are not enough.

TRUCKERS ONBOARD

Six seamen stood at intervals along the deck to ensure that the rigs were parked correctly. The rule is to fit as many vehicles as possible on the ship.

Every meter of deckspace is worth money. A few more rigs packed into the hold means a lot to the shipping line. Maybe the mate gets a slap on the back for a job well-done when it's all over, who knows?

'Closer! Come Closer!' yelled the mate. He'd turned his job into a veritable one-man-sideshow. Leaving any space at all is unacceptable. To him, forgetting to fold your mirrors in was the same as holding a certificate of idiocy!

There were still a couple of meters left in some of the lanes. To us it looked like enough space for three or four cars. That mate managed to fit seven more cars!

We caught sight of a brown Volvo running like a greyhound towards the ferry. He didn't stand a chance. The mighty steel ramp had already started inching its way upwards. There was no room left in the gigantic floating parking lot!

Some Scandinavian who could do

with a taste of cold beer and the feel of cool crisp sheets. Probably beside himself with homesickness. We could almost hear his frustrated cries.

While the bone-tired trucker slept it off in his cabin, and our disappointed Volvo driver swore at his misfortune, the dining room slowly filled up with tired truckers — the buffet was probably a Godsend; after mile upon mile of greasy coffee at roadside diners, the food tasted heavenly!

The scene was to say the least, unique.

Roedby — Puttgarden, Halskov — Knudshoeved, Esbjerg — Harwich, Fredrikshavn — Gothenburg, Stockholm — Helsinki, these are just a few of the vital arteries where wheels are not enough. Here the ferries are extremely vital links that spew forth their trucks and cargoes 24 hours a day, every day.

Travemünde — Trelleborg isn't among the longer links, but isn't one of the shortest, either.

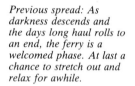

Previous spread: As darkness descends and the days long haul rolls to an end, the ferry is a welcomed phase. At last a chance to stretch out and relax for awhile.

(Below) One after another the trucks are being guided into the ferry. The tighter they park, the better.

(Above) 'Too much red-tape!' Exclaimed one intercontinental trucker. On the ferry one gets a good chance to check the documents in peace and quiet.

(Left) To be in command of a ferry is no Sunday excursion. A skilled staff is needed to handle these big vessels properly.

Over:

(Top) The trucker's life would be a lot different if there were no ferries. The long hauls down from northern Europe to the Arab world would hardly have been possible.

(Left) Every single inch of deck space is used. A good mate can direct and organize the loading of rigs so that no space is spared.

(Right) The trucks must be tied down in case the ferry runs into stormy seas.

TRUCKERS ONBOARD

After a warm and relaxing night, one is revitalised eager to continue on wheels.

'It's different between night and day', Rolf, a trucker from Stockholm, told us. 'To ride over on the ferry during the day seems like wasted time; yet at night, it feels like a real time-saver!'

Rolf raised his foaming tankard of beer appreciatively. He was in no hurry for bed!

'I've been running around on the Continent for a couple of weeks now. I've run this trade for as long as I can remember, seems like. It's always just as great to while away some of the hours just talking with the other boys along the route.'

Several of the others nodded their heads in agreement.

'First trip over, well everything was new,' sighed one of the truckers at the table. 'But if you've run up and down here for awhile, well, it gets downright boring. Sure, you have time to rest while on board, but it just takes too long.'

There was the sound of tinkling glass from the bar. A couple of truckers were still managing to stay upright; the noise was mostly coming from vacationers who didn't have somebody else's freight to worry about.

An hour or so later, the dining room was practically empty. The jumbo ferry pounded along its northerly route, adjusted a degree here or there by the tireless computer. We were left with the empty glasses and the personnel.

We were awakened at 6.30 am by the

TRUCKERS ONBOARD

sound of music blasting out of cracked speakers. The ship slowly crawled back to life. In the kitchen they were wide awake, the stress of breakfast — preparing for this is hectic to say the least! Several hundred newly awakened and hungry passengers waiting to be fed!

Midnight snacks are fine, but breakfast is the most important meal on the ship. Tea, coffee, fresh-baked bread, cheese, ham, omelettes, hard-boiled eggs, soft-boiled eggs — this breakfast doesn't have to bow down to any five-star hotel!

Truckers are privileged — they don't have to stand in line. The Liner Company looks after its best customers. A coffee/tea preparer stood ready in a special department.

'That's just the way it should be!' Rolf exclaimed. Even though he was among the last out of the bar last night, he looked fresh as a daisy.

'They know where they make their living from', he snorted.

We basely recognized him as the same guy from last night. His T-shirt had been changed for a plaid flannel shirt, his stubble was gone, and his jeans seemed to have won the first round of the day with his middle! He reeked of Brut, and his eyes were quick, sharp. Two hard-boiled eggs followed by a large hunk of omelette washed down with two large mugs of coffee, and Knud Joergensen was back in the real world.

Over: The trucks are important to the ferry lines. Truckers are treated with respect. They have their own serving areas and sometimes even a sauna.

TRUCKERS ONBOARD

'Man, was I ever tired! I've been out six weeks. Coming up from Jeddah, in Saudi Arabia, and headed for Sundsvall, up in Northern Sweden.'

Knud's been driving for almost 15 years now. He got tired of the life aboard the ferries a long time ago. He lit a cigarette and exhaled the smoke slowly.

'The best part of it all is when you reach your home turf and can lay your hands on a real live honest-to-goodness cigarette worth smoking,' he said.

'Down there, seems like all they got is some weird seaweed the camels peed on!' We all laughed.

'But up in these boats, this is paradise! If I hadn't missed the ferry between Tartus, Syria, and Koper in Yugoslavia, I'd be dead probably, though! She sank just out of Cyprus with 150 trucks on board. I reached that boarding ramp ten minutes too late!'

Knud had planned to be back in Denmark within four days. But he had one more ferry route before he reached home, Gothenburg—Fredrikshavn.

'If I'm lucky, I'd get a couple of weeks at home with the wife and kids. Then, off we'd go again! Maybe it'd be to Saudi Arabia again, who knows?'

Somebody mumbled some meaningless jibberish through the loudspeakers. The rattle and clash of the cash registers at the duty-free shops drowned every other noise. Knud and his buddies didn't make a move. They're old hands, they know

First, the ramp has to be lowered and secured. Then it's off you go for all the autos. Then, and only then, the trucks roll off the ship. There's lots of time and no panic.

Twenty minutes later we heard the first sounds of the diesels below us thundering into life. We could see the long line of trucks snaking into Sweden from the ship's hold. In just a few minutes they were spread all over southern Sweden in a widening pattern. Trucking everywhere in order that the machinery of modern life can keep ticking another day.

Up in the ship they were already preparing for the next load of trucks and travellers bound in the opposite direction. Cabins cleaned, beds made. Fresh produce brought on board. Fresh water pumped in from the side. New blood into the vital link.

Sometimes, we need more than just wheels . . . .

(Above) The mate is a master when it comes to packing rigs into the limited space available. Every rig means a jingle from the cash register.

(Left) Most ferries are for trucks. They are the main source of income for some ferry lines.

Over: The trucker who makes it in time to the ferry can heave a sigh of relief. No time lost in waiting for the next ferry to arrive.

TRUCKERS ONBOARD

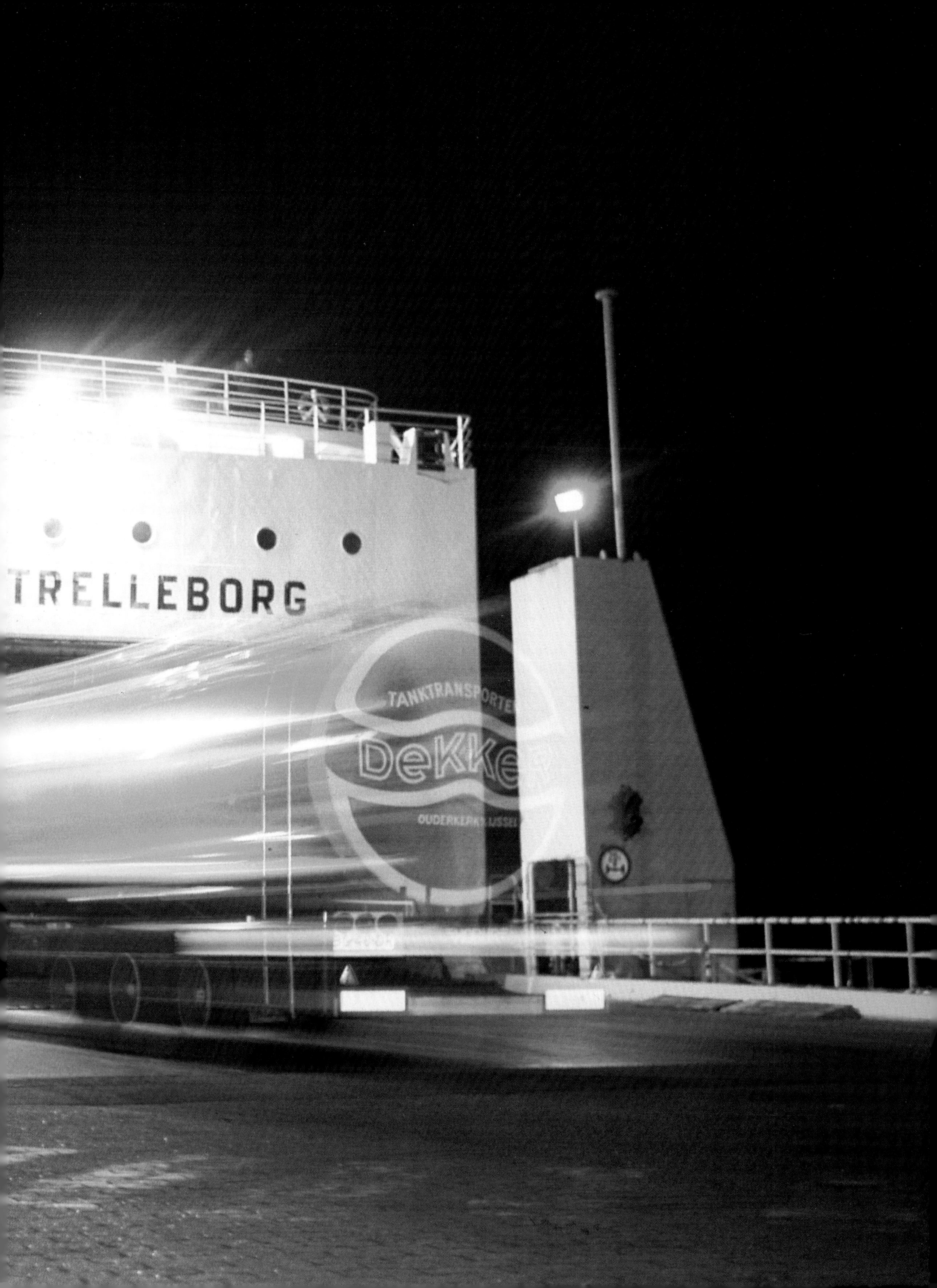
TRELLEBORG

chapter 12

INDIAN AFFAIR

The racket tearing from the cassette deck made me nervous.

The Indian folk music and the screaming of tortured engines, were mixed together with the constant blaring and honking of horns. I was beginning to wonder if we would ever reach our destination.

Our driver and I had gotten acquainted earlier. I could see that he wasn't in any great rush. We had left Srinagar, capital of the Indian state of Jammu-Kashmir earlier that morning.

The town is criss-crossed by waterways and canals along which the 'shikaras' smoothly slide, bobbing softly on the current, like some twisted Venetian scene. Along the banks poplars, weeping willows, cherry, and apple trees, swing softly to the breeze.

I was a little worried about the trip. The Kashmir valley, which lies between the masses of Karakoa and the Himalayas, is often smittened by landslides, and the road down to the Indian plains is often completely impassable!

The Kashmir valley is usually inaccessible during winter. The torrents of rain flatten practically everything in their path, bringing down telephone lines and grounding air traffic.

We stopped. A small boy, perhaps ten years old, was squatting by the roadside and quickly boiled up some liquid. It tasted like hot sugar-water, but was in fact, according to our driver, a cup of tea!

For less than one rupee, hardly a few cents, I washed down three cups. I'd still not dared to drink the Indian 'fresh' water, although I was dying of thirst. My stomach had already made itself felt a couple of times.

After a few minutes chatter at this Indian 'truckstop', we climbed aboard and began our jostling, bouncing journey once again.

It only took me a few hours of sitting beside Singh to fully grasp the way that Indian traffic work. It all hangs on the horn! Whoever honks loudest and longest gets furthest.

Indian trucks do not carry many accessories. But an extra heavy-duty air horn is standard.

No road-courtesy exists on the Indian roads. Nobody will allow another to get ahead. So, you just lean on that horn and blast your way past.

After two hours in the shaking and rattling cab we had managed a bare 20 kilometers... the traffic outside the city was as intense as in the downtown area.

(Above) Repairs are often carried out in the open. And why not park in some river, where it's cool and fresh. Chance to wash up as well.

(Left) Tatatrucks are the most common ones in India. They are manufactured under license from Mercedes.

Over:

The overloads are numerous, though not all of them are as precarious as these.

INDIAN AFFAIR

(Above) All that
separates this convoy
from the drop are loose
concrete slabs precarious-
ly lining the cliff edge.

(Right) In less traf-
ficked areas one usually
come across the slums. Not
many deliveries to these
areas but many drivers have
their homes here.

(Far right top) An Indian
driver: 'I am happy with
what I have'.

(Far right bottom) The
Indian way of parking
buses.

INDIAN
AFFAIR

Everywhere there were crowds of people, bicycles, bullock carts, horses and the holy cattle. Singh steered a zig-zag course through the throngs, constantly pounding on his horn.

It didn't seem to matter which side of the road one drove on.

According to the police, there are about 10,000 trucks in the province of Jammu-Kashmir, almost all of which have a single rear-axle.

Trailers are a rarity, as suitable roads and highways don't exist. Any tractor-trailer combination wouldn't get very far!

Most of the rigs are shaken to pieces by the terrible roads, and it really is a miracle that they hold up at all!

Our goal was the town of Jammu, 300 kilometers from Srinagar. At our speed, it seemed a long way off!

An hour later, with a few more miles behind us, it was time for another pit-stop. Two small boys came crawling out of a hut by the side of the road, dragging a couple of Jerry cans and a funnel! Singh ordered the boys to fill the tank. There aren't any diesel pumps along the road to Jammu!

I must have dozed off because when I opened my eyes we'd reached the small village of Islamabad, 56 kilometers south of Srinagar. It was almost twelve and high time for lunch!

Singh called it a restaurant . . . what we

Over:

(Left top) High pressure waterjets and other conveniences are not necessary in India. You wash directly in the river.

(Left bottom) The roads are dusty — as long as they are dry. But when the rain comes they become mud pools.

(Right) An Indian driver often has to make the repairs himself. Where else but in the river.

INDIAN AFFAIR

westerners might call this 'road-house' is hard to say exactly — it's a matter of opinion whether or not we could even use the word 'house'.

I was still fighting a losing battle with my stomach, but I knew I had to at least swallow a few mouthfuls of the reddish mush that was set down before me. If for no other reason, simply because it was polite.

Let me ask you, have you ever tried to put out a bonfire with a bottle of soda pop?

After pouring two bottles down my tortured throat, I was innocently told that all the hottest pepper had been picked out especially for me. I gripped my poor stomach with both hands and breathed a silent prayer that the dynamite I'd just dumped down my throat would at least blast the bacteria to smithereens down there.

We had just reached the outskirts of

the village when Singh jammed the the brakes on hard — by the side of the road were about 10 to 20 soldiers hitch-hiking. Singh gave the whole bunch a free ride. Weapons, ammunition, packs, were all heaved up on to the rig. We had hardly moved off again before the whole group dozed off into a fitful sleep.

The road began to twist and turn on its way up into the mountains, and we were soon crawling along at less than 20 kph but that engine was working overtime all the same.

There were no guardrails along the roadside. Just a few blocks of granite that had been thrown down here and there along the route, which ran right along the sheer drop of the mountain's cliffsides!

After going uphill for a few hours, we reached a tunnel. It is a vital link to Srinagar.

An earthquake, or even a landslide,

INDIAN AFFAIR

(Far left) What traffic rules? Chaos often reigns on city roads.

(Left) A lonesome policeman can scarcely direct the messy traffic. But he does his best.

(Below bottom) At a border checkpoint.

Over: Men behind the wheels. Simplicity and the belief in religion. The turbans are symbols of the Sikh faith.

would quickly and effectively put an end to all access by land to the south of the city of Srinagar. She'd be isolated, cut off from the outside except for air traffic.

Without consulting Singh, I yanked out my camera to take some quick snaps, but I'd hardly managed to raise the lens before I found myself staring down the cold dark barrels of several machine-guns.

I quite quickly realized my mistake — 70 kilometers north lay Pakistan. This is a sensitive region and the tunnel is well guarded at every point.

I ended up having to explain my behaviour to an officer whose exact rank I never managed to establish. He had a lot of brass on his uniform anyway!

After they had torn out two films from my cameras, even though I explained that I'd had no chance as yet to take any shots, mercy finally came before justice. I was allowed to go free, provided I promised never to do such a stupid thing again!

I crawled back up into the cab, a shaken man. We eased our way through the kilometer long tunnel, and as we came out the other side, I saw that we had made

it to the mountain's highest point, and now only had the downhill stretch to face.

So far we'd not made as many miles as hours on this trip, and I seriously considered walking down the long slope instead of riding. But I couldn't hurt Singh's feelings.

The brake tracks point straight down along the road and spoke for themselves. Small stone walls along the sides of the roads had fallen apart and beyond them was an empty, airy nothing. Far below us the valley floor stretched into the distance.

Singh didn't even react to any of this. He double-clutched and double-clutched his way down. I shut my eyes!

At about nine o'clock that evening we reached Jammu. Singh had pushed his Tata to breath-taking speeds of 70 km/h on a couple of clear stretches!

Our 300 kilometer journey had taken us 14 hours. Tired, sweaty and aching, I stumbled down from the cab and said goodbye to Singh.

I had gotten a good idea of what it's like to be a trucker, to wrangle rigs, through the snarl that is India today.

*(— Above —)
Up in the mountains at Kashmir the roads are often only wide enough for one vehicle to.*

(Left top) To an Indian driver, as it is to his western counterparts, it is important to keep the truck clean.

(Left bottom) The water transports are an important part of the industy.

Over:

(Left) The motifs are often of very high standards, sometimes comparable to those on American trucks.

(Right top) Trucks await to be unloaded.

(Right bottom) The water is supposed to be used for watering dusty roads, but is not bad if someone wants to wash his truck.

INDIAN AFFAIR

TRUCKING AROUND THE WORLD

TRUCKING
INTERNATIONAL

Project Manager:
Ty Fong

Text:
Lars-Magnus Jansson
Sture Bergendahl
Pelle Andersson
Kent Andersson

Photographers:
Christer Johansson, Torsten Berglund, Sture Bergendahl,
Mike Key, Tony Murray, Niels Jansen, Tor Hansson, Anders
Albinsson, Ove Gehrmann, Jan Alexandersson, Torbjörn
Hansson, Pelle Andersson, Henrik Saxgren, Francis Reyes,
Razjivine, Gert Homeltz, Björn Carlsson.

Layout:
Thomas Daleke
Ty Fong

Translators:
Robert Scattergood
Appelgren & Mattisson

A special thanks to typesetters: Ann-Christin Högström,
Anne-Marie Lagerholm, Anita Ringkvist and Anne-Marie
Håkansson for their patience; as well as Anders Andersson
and Inger Holgersson whose help with the technical
production had been invaluable.

And a very special thanks to Stig L. Sjöberg, the publisher
of TRUCKING International and TRAILER magazines,
without whose fatherly support and advise this book would
not have been possible, and to Göran Daleke, Manager of
Förlags AB Albinsson & Sjöberg, Sweden.